MTEL 13

Biology
Teacher Certification Exam

By: Sharon Wynne, M.S
Southern Connecticut State University

"And, while there's no reason yet to panic, I think it's only prudent that we make preparations to panic."

XAMonline, INC.
Boston

XAMonline, Inc.
21 Orient Ave.
Melrose, MA 02176
Toll Free 1-800-509-4128
Email: winwin1111@aol.com
Web www.xamonline.com
Fax: 1-718-662-9268

Library of Congress Cataloging-in-Publication Data

Wynne, Sharon A.
   Biology 013: Teacher Certification / Sharon A. Wynne. -2nd ed.
   ISBN 978-1-58197-844-1
      1. Biology 013.   2. Study Guides.   3. MTEL
      4. Teachers' Certification & Licensure.   5. Careers

Disclaimer:
The material presented in this publication is the sole work of XAMonline and was created independently from the National Education Association, Educational Testing Service, or any State Department of Education, National Evaluation Systems or other testing affiliates.

Between the time of publication and printing, state specific standards, testing formats, and website information may change. XAMonline developed the sample test questions and they reflect content similar to real tests; however, they are not former tests. XAMonline assembles content that aligns with state standards, but makes no claims nor guarantees regarding test performance. Numerical scores are determined by testing companies such as NES or ETS and then are compared with individual state standards. A passing score varies from state to state.

Printed in the United States of America   œ - 1, 07

MTEL: Biology 13
ISBN: 978-1-58197-687-8

Table of Contents

Great Study and Testing Tips!

What to study in order to prepare for the subject assessments is the focus of this study guide, but equally important is *how* you study.

You can increase your chances of truly mastering the information by taking some simple, but effective steps.

Study Tips:

1. **Some foods aid the learning process.** Foods such as milk, nuts, seeds, rice, and oats help your study efforts by releasing natural memory enhancers called CCKs (*cholecystokinins*) composed of *tryptophan*, *choline*, and *phenylalanine*. All of these chemicals enhance the neurotransmitters associated with memory. Before studying, try a light, protein-rich meal of eggs, turkey, and fish. All of these foods release the memory enhancing chemicals. The better the connections, the more you comprehend.

Likewise, before you take a test, stick to a light snack of energy boosting and relaxing foods. A glass of milk, a piece of fruit, or some peanuts all release various memory-boosting chemicals and help you relax and focus on the subject at hand.

2. **Learn to take great notes.** A by-product of our modern culture is that we have grown accustomed to getting our information in short doses (e.g., TV news sound bites or USA Today style newspaper articles).

Consequently, we've subconsciously trained ourselves to assimilate information better in neat little packages. If your notes are scrawled all over the paper, it fragments the flow of information. Strive for clarity. Newspapers use a standard format to achieve clarity. Your notes can be much clearer through use of proper formatting. A very effective format is called the *"Cornell Method."*

> Take a sheet of loose-leaf lined notebook paper and draw a line all the way down the paper about 1-2" from the left-hand edge.

> Draw another line across the width of the paper about 1-2" up from the bottom. Repeat this process on the reverse side of the page.

Look at the highly effective result. You have ample room for notes, a left hand margin for special emphasis items or inserting supplementary data from the textbook, a large area at the bottom for a brief summary, and a little rectangular space for just about anything you want.

3. **Get the concept then the details.** Too often we focus on the details and fail to gather an understanding of the concept. If you simply memorize dates, places, and names, you may well miss the whole point of the subject.

Putting concepts in your own words can increase your understanding. If you are working from a textbook, automatically summarize each paragraph in your mind. If you are outlining text, don't simply copy the author's words, *rephrase* them in your own words.

You remember your own thoughts and words much better than someone else's, and subconsciously tend to associate the important details to the core concepts.

4. **Ask Why?** Pull apart written material paragraph by paragraph and don't forget the captions under the illustrations.

Example: If the heading is "Stream Erosion", flip it around to read "Why do streams erode?" Then answer the question.

If you train your mind to think in a series of questions and answers, not only will you learn more, but you will decrease your test anxiety by increasing your familiarity with the question and answer process.

5. **Read for reinforcement and future needs.** Even if you only have ten minutes, put your notes or a book in your hand. Your mind is similar to a computer, you have to input data in order to process it. *By reading, you are creating the neural connections for future retrieval.* The more times you read something, the more you reinforce the learning of ideas.

Even if you don't fully understand something on the first pass, *your mind stores much of the material for later recall.*

6. **Relax to learn so go into exile.** Our bodies respond to an inner clock called biorhythms. Burning the midnight oil works well for some people, but not everyone.

If possible, set aside a particular place to study that is free of distractions. Shut off the television, cell phone, and pager and exile your friends and family during your study period.

If silence really bothers you, try background music. Light classical music at a low volume has been shown to aid in concentration. Music that evokes pleasant emotions without lyrics is highly suggested. Try just about anything by Mozart. It relaxes you.

7. Use arrows not highlighters. At best, it's difficult to read a page full of yellow, pink, blue, and green streaks. Try staring at a neon sign for a while and you'll soon see that the horde of colors obscure the message.

A quick note, a brief dash of color, an underline, and an arrow pointing to a particular passage is much clearer than a horde of highlighted words.

8. Budget your study time. Although you shouldn't ignore any of the material, *allocate your available study time in the same ratio that topics may appear on the test.*

Testing Tips:

1. <u>Get smart, play dumb</u>. Don't read anything into the question. Don't make an assumption that the test writer is looking for something else than what is asked.

2. <u>Read the question and all the choices *twice* before answering the question</u>. You may miss something by not carefully reading and re-reading both the question and the answers.

If you really don't have a clue as to the right answer, leave it blank the first time through. Go on to the other questions, as they may provide a clue as to how to answer the skipped questions.

If later on you still can't answer the skipped ones . . . ***Guess.*** The only penalty for guessing is that you *might* get it wrong. Only one thing is certain; if you don't put anything down, you will get it wrong!

3. <u>Turn the question into a statement</u>. Look at the wording of the questions. The syntax of the question usually provides a clue. Does it seem more familiar as a statement rather than as a question? Does it sound strange?

By turning a question into a statement, you may be able to spot if an answer sounds right, and it may also trigger memories of material you have read.

4. <u>Look for hidden clues</u>. It's actually very difficult to compose multiple-foil (choice) questions without giving away part of the answer in the options presented.

In most multiple-choice questions you can often readily eliminate one or two of the potential answers. This leaves you with only two real possibilities and automatically your odds become fifty-fifty with very little work.

5. <u>Trust your instincts</u>. On questions that you aren't really certain about, go with your basic instincts. **Your first impression on how to answer a question is usually correct.**

6. <u>Mark your answers directly on the test booklet</u>. Don't bother trying to fill in the optical scan sheet on the first pass through the test.

Just be very careful not to mismark your answers when you eventually transcribe them to the scan sheet.

7. <u>Watch the clock</u>! You have a set amount of time to answer the questions. Don't get bogged down trying to answer a single question at the expense of 10 questions you can more readily answer.

THIS PAGE BLANK

Subarea I.   Scientific Inquiry

0001   Apply procedures for gathering, organizing, interpreting, evaluating, and communicating data

Methods or procedures for collecting data

The procedure used to obtain data is important to the outcome. Experiments consist of **controls** and **variables**. A control is the experiment run under normal, unmanipulated conditions.

A variable is a factor or condition the scientist manipulates. In biology, the variable may be light, temperature, pH, time, etc. Scientists can use the differences in tested variables to make predictions or form hypotheses. Only one variable should be tested at a time. In other words, one would not alter both the temperature and pH of the experimental subject.

An **independent variable** is one is the researcher directly changes or manipulates. This could be the amount of light given to a plant or the temperature at which bacteria is grown. The **dependent variable** is the factor that changes due to the influence of the independent variable.

Appropriate measuring devices

The most common instrument used for measuring volume is the graduated cylinder. The standard unit of measurement is milliliters (mL). To ensure accurate measurement, it is important to read the liquid in the cylinder at the bottom of the meniscus, the curved surface of the liquid.

The most common instrument used for measuring mass is the triple beam balance. The triple beam balance can accurately measure tenths of a gram and can estimate hundredths of a gram.

The ruler and meter stick are the most commonly used instruments for measuring length. As with all scientific measurements, standard units of length are metric.

The metric system

The **metric system** is the most accepted system of scientific measurement worldwide. Scientists use the metric system because it allows easier comparison of experimental results produced by scientists around the world.

The meter is the basic metric unit of length. One meter is 1.1 yards. The liter is the basic metric unit of volume. 3.846 liters is 1 gallon. The gram is the basic metric unit of mass. 1000 grams is 2.2 pounds.

The following prefixes define multiples of the basic metric units.

deca- 10X the base unit
hecto- 100X the base unit
kilo- 1,000X the base unit
mega- 1,000,000X the base unit
giga- 1,000,000,000X the base unit

deci - 1/10 the base unit
centi - 1/100 the base unit
milli - 1/1,000 the base unit
micro- 1/1,000,000 the base unit
nano- 1/1,000,000,000 the base unit

tera- 1,000,000,000,000X the base unit

pico- 1/1,000,000,000,000 the base unit

Knowledge of appropriate and effective graphic representation of data

The type of graphic representation used to present results depends on the type of data collected. **Line graphs** compare different sets of related data and help predict data. For example, a line graph could compare the rate of activity of different enzymes at varying temperatures. A **bar graph** or **histogram** compares different items and helps make comparisons based on the data. For example, a bar graph could compare the ages of children in a classroom. A **pie chart** is useful when organizing data as part of a whole. For example, a pie chart could display the percent of time students spend on various after school activities.

Knowledge of labeling graphs with independent and dependent variables

The independent variable is placed on the x-axis (horizontal axis) and the dependent variable is placed on the y-axis (vertical axis). It is important to choose the appropriate units for labeling the axes. It is best to divide the largest value to be plotted by the number of blocks on the graph, and round to the nearest whole number.

0002 Apply principles and procedures of research and experimental design

The Scientific Method

The first step in scientific inquiry is posing a question. Next, a hypothesis is formed to provide a plausible explanation. An experiment is then proposed and performed to test this hypothesis. A comparison between the predicted and observed results is the next step. Conclusions are then formed and it is determined whether the hypothesis is correct or incorrect. If incorrect, the next step is to form a new hypothesis and repeat the process.

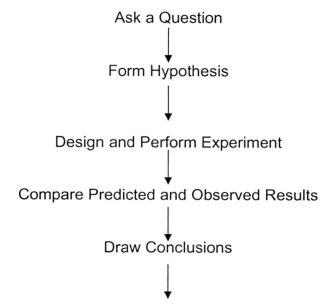

Ask a Question

↓

Form Hypothesis

↓

Design and Perform Experiment

↓

Compare Predicted and Observed Results

↓

Draw Conclusions

↓

Form New Hypothesis and Repeat (if necessary)

Processes by which scientists generate and test hypotheses

Science is a body of knowledge systematically derived from study, observation, and experimentation. Its goal is to identify and establish principles and theories that may be applied to solve problems.

Scientific experimentation must be repeatable. Experimentation results in theories that can be disproved and changed. Science depends on communication, agreement, and disagreement among scientists. It is composed of theories, laws, and hypotheses.

> **Theory -** principles or relationships which have been verified and accepted.

> **Law -** an explanation of events that occur with uniformity under the same conditions (laws of nature, law of gravitation).

Hypothesis - an unproved theory or educated guess followed by research to best explain a phenomena. A theory is a proven hypothesis.

Science is limited by the available technology. An example of this would be the relationship between the discovery of the cell and the invention of the microscope. As our technology improves, more hypotheses will become theories and possibly laws. The ability to collect data also limits scientific discovery. Scientists may interpret data differently on different occasions. These limitations mean that scientific explanations are changeable as new technologies emerge.

0003 Apply procedures related to the proper use of tools, equipment, and materials (including chemicals and living organisms) commonly used in biology, and practices for maintaining safety during biological investigations.

Knowledge of appropriate use of laboratory materials, tools, and equipment

Light microscopes are commonly used in high school laboratory experiments. Total magnification is the magnification of the ocular times the magnification of the objective lens. Oculars usually magnify 10X and objective lenses usually magnify 10X on low and 40X on high.

Procedures for the care and use of microscopes include:

- cleaning all lenses with lens paper only
- carrying microscopes with two hands (one on the arm and one on the base)
- always beginning on low power when focusing before switching to high power
- storing microscopes with the low power objective down
- always using a coverslip when viewing wet mount slides
- bringing the objective down to its lowest position when focusing and moving up to avoid breaking the slide or scratching the lens

To prepare **wet mount slides**, place a drop of water on the specimen and put a glass coverslip on top of the drop of water. Dropping the coverslip at a forty-five degree angle will help avoid air bubbles.

Chromatography uses the principles of capillarity to separate substances such as plant pigments. Molecules of a larger size will move slower up the paper, whereas smaller molecules will move more quickly producing lines of pigment.

An **indicator** is any substance used to assist in the classification of another substance. An example of an indicator is litmus paper. Litmus paper is a way to measure whether a substance is acidic or basic. Blue litmus turns pink when an acid is placed on it and pink litmus turns blue when a base is placed on it. pH paper is a more accurate measure of pH, with the paper turning different colors depending on the pH value.

Spectrophotometry measures percent of light at different wavelengths absorbed and transmitted by a pigment solution.

Centrifugation involves spinning substances at a high speed. The more dense part of a solution will settle to the bottom of the test tube, while the lighter material will stay on top. Centrifugation is used to separate blood into blood cells and plasma, with the heavier blood cells settling to the bottom.

Electrophoresis uses electrical charges of molecules to separate them according to their size. The molecules, such as DNA or proteins, are pulled through a gel towards either the positive end of the gel box (if the material has a negative charge) or the negative end of the gel box (if the material has a positive charge). DNA is negatively charged and moves towards the positive charge.

Storing, identifying, and disposing of chemicals and biological materials

All laboratory solutions should be prepared as directed in the lab manual. Care should be taken to avoid contamination. All glassware should be rinsed thoroughly with distilled water before using and cleaned well after use. All solutions should be made with distilled water as tap water contains dissolved particles that may affect the results of an experiment. Unused solutions should be disposed of according to local disposal procedures.

The "Right to Know Law" covers science teachers who work with potentially hazardous chemicals. Briefly, the law states that employees must be informed of potentially toxic chemicals. An inventory must be made available if requested. The inventory must contain information about the hazards and properties of the chemicals. This inventory is to be checked against the "Substance List". Training must be provided on safe handling and interpretation of the Material Safety Data Sheet.

The following chemicals are potential carcinogens and not allowed in school facilities: Acrylonitriel, Arsenic compounds, Asbestos, Bensidine, Benzene, Cadmium compounds, Chloroform, Chromium compounds, Ethylene oxide, Ortho-toluidine, Nickle powder, and Mercury.

Chemicals should not be stored on bench tops or near heat sources. They should be stored in groups based on their reactivity with one another and in protective storage cabinets. All containers within the lab must be labeled. Suspected and known carcinogens must be labeled as such and stored in trays to contain leaks and spills.

Chemical waste should be disposed of in properly labeled containers. Waste should be separated based on its reactivity with other chemicals.

Biological material should never be stored near food or water used for human consumption. All biological material should be appropriately labeled. All blood and body fluids should be put in a well-contained container with a secure lid to prevent leaking. All biological waste should be disposed of in biological hazardous waste bags.

Material safety data sheets are available for every chemical and biological substance. These are available directly from the distribution company and the internet. Before using lab equipment, all lab workers should read and understand the equipment manuals.

Use of live specimens

No dissections may be performed on living mammalian vertebrates or birds. Lower order life and invertebrates may be used. Biological experiments may be done with all animals except mammalian vertebrates or birds. No physiological harm may result to the animal. All animals housed and cared for in the school must be handled in a safe and humane manner. Animals are not to remain on school premises during extended vacations unless adequate care is provided. Any instructor who intentionally refuses to comply with the laws may be suspended or dismissed.

Pathogenic organisms must never be used for experimentation. Students should adhere to the following rules at all times when working with microorganisms to avoid accidental contamination:

1. Treat all microorganisms as if they were pathogenic.
2. Maintain sterile conditions at all times.

Dissection and alternatives to dissection

Animals which were not obtained from recognized sources should not be used. Decaying animals or those of unknown origin may harbor pathogens and/or parasites. Specimens should be rinsed before handling. Latex gloves are recommended. If not available, students with sores or scratches should be excused from the activity. Formaldehyde is likely carcinogenic and should be avoided or disposed of according to district regulations. Students objecting to dissections for moral reasons should be given an alternative assignment. Interactive dissections are available online or from software companies for those students who object to performing dissections. There should be no penalty for those students who refuse to physically perform a dissection.

Laboratory safety procedures

All science labs should contain the following **safety equipment**.

- Fire blanket that is visible and accessible
- Ground Fault Circuit Interrupters (GFCI) within two feet of water supplies
- Signs designating room exits
- Emergency shower providing a continuous flow of water
- Emergency eye wash station that can be activated by the foot or forearm
- Eye protection for every student
- A means of sanitizing equipment
- Emergency exhaust fans providing ventilation to the outside of the building
- Master cut-off switches for gas, electric, and compressed air. Switches must have permanently attached handles. Cut-off switches must be clearly labeled
- An ABC fire extinguisher
- Storage cabinets for flammable materials
- Chemical spill control kit
- Fume hood with a motor that is spark proof
- Protective laboratory aprons made of flame retardant material
- Signs that will alert of potential hazardous conditions
- Labeled containers for broken glassware, flammables, corrosives, and waste

Students should wear safety goggles when performing dissections, heating, or while using acids and bases. Hair should always be tied back and objects should never be placed in the mouth. Food should not be consumed while in the laboratory. Hands should always be washed before and after laboratory experiments. In case of an accident, eye washes and showers should be used for eye contamination or a chemical spill that covers the student's body. Small chemical spills should only be contained and cleaned by the teacher. Kitty litter or a chemical spill kit should be used to clean a spill. For large spills, the school administration and the local fire department should be notified. Biological spills should only be handled by the teacher. Contamination with biological waste can be cleaned by using bleach when appropriate. Accidents and injuries should always be reported to the school administration and local health facilities. The severity of the accident or injury will determine the course of action.

It is the responsibility of the teacher to provide a safe environment for his or her students. Proper supervision greatly reduces the risk of injury and a teacher should never leave a class for any reason without providing alternate supervision. After an accident, two factors are considered, **foreseeability** and **negligence**. Foreseeability is the anticipation that an event may occur under certain circumstances. Negligence is the failure to exercise ordinary or reasonable care. Safety procedures should be a part of the science curriculum and a well managed classroom is important to avoid potential lawsuits.

0004   Understand historical and social aspects of biological study and contributions made to biology by various people.

Key events in the history of biological study

Anton van Leeuwenhoek is known as the father of microscopy. In the 1650s, Leeuwenhoek began making tiny lenses that produced magnifications up to 300x. He was the first to see and describe bacteria, yeast plants, and the microscopic life found in water. Over the years, light microscopes have advanced to produce greater clarity and magnification. The scanning electron microscope (SEM) was developed in the 1950s. Instead of light, a beam of electrons passes through the specimen. Scanning electron microscopes have a resolution about one thousand times greater than light microscopes. The disadvantage of the SEM is that the chemical and physical methods used to prepare the sample result in the death of the specimen.

In the late 1800s, Louis Pasteur discovered the role of microorganisms in the cause of disease, pasteurization, and the rabies vaccine. Robert Koch took this observation one step further by formulating a theory that specific pathogens caused specific diseases. Scientists still use **Koch's postulates** as guidelines in the field of microbiology. The guidelines state that all of the following criteria must be met to show that a microbe causes a disease.

1. The same pathogen must be found in every diseased organism but not in healthy organisms.
2. The pathogen must be isolated and grown in culture.
3. The pathogen must induce disease in experimental organisms.
4. The same pathogen must be isolated from the experimental organism.

The discovery of the structure of DNA was another key event in biological study. In the 1950s, James Watson and Francis Crick identified the structure of a DNA molecule as that of a double helix. This structure made it possible to explain DNA's ability to replicate and to control the synthesis of proteins.

The use of animals in biological research has expedited many scientific discoveries. Animal research has allowed scientists to learn more about animal biological systems, including the circulatory and reproductive systems. One significant use of animals is for the testing of drugs, vaccines, and other products (such as perfumes and shampoos) before use or consumption by humans.

The debate about the ethical treatment of animals has been ongoing since the introduction of animals in research. Many people believe the use of animals in research is cruel and unnecessary. Animal use is federally and locally regulated. The purpose of the Institutional Animal Care and Use Committee (IACUC) is to oversee and evaluate all aspects of an institution's animal care and use program.

The impact of social factors on biological study

Society as a whole impacts biological research. Societal pressure has led to bans and restrictions on human cloning research. The United States government and the governments of many other countries have restricted human cloning. The U.S. legislature has banned the use of federal funds for the development of human cloning techniques. Some individual states have banned human cloning regardless of where the funds originate.

The demand for genetically modified crops by society and industry has steadily increased over the years. Genetic engineering in the agricultural field has led to improved crops for human use and consumption. Crops are genetically modified for increased growth and insect resistance because of the demand for larger and greater quantities of produce.

With advances in biotechnology come those in society who oppose it. Ethical questions come into play when discussing animal and human research. Does it need to be done? What are the effects on humans and animals? There are no absolute right or wrong answers to these questions. There are governmental agencies in place to regulate the use of humans and animals for research.

Science and technology are often referred to as a "double-edged sword". Although advances in medicine have greatly improved the quality and length of life, certain moral and ethical controversies have arisen. Unforeseen environmental problems may result from technological advances. Advances in science have led to an improved economy through biotechnology as applied to agriculture, yet it has put our health care system at risk and has caused the cost of medical care to skyrocket. Society depends on science, yet is necessary that the public be scientifically literate and informed in order to allow potentially unethical procedures to occur. Especially vulnerable are the areas of genetic research and fertility. It is important for science teachers to stay abreast of current research and to involve students in critical thinking and ethics whenever possible.

0005 Understand the interrelationships between biology, society, technology, and other sciences and disciplines.

Math, science, and technology share many common themes. All three use models, diagrams, and graphs to simplify a concept for analysis and interpretation. Patterns observed in these systems lead to predictions based on these observations.

Biology, science, technology, and other sciences and disciplines are interconnected. Teaching biology requires the incorporation of other areas of science as well as other disciplines. It is very difficult to separate these areas and that's why an integrated approach to teaching and learning is becoming more and more common and popular. For example, we can't make a graph without using some mathematical skills involving calculations.

Biology is an everyday experience. It involves life and the relationships of living things and as we are all a part of life, it is much more relevant and interesting to us. Society uses science and technology in numerous ways. Society also uses the knowledge and the technological advances made for its benefit. A basic understanding of all these disciplines makes any society well informed and knowledgeable. The advances in science using high end technology is making it possible to know or choose the sex of the baby in advance and some people are making decisions based on that information. *In vitro* fertilization is another advance in technology that is becoming very popular and useful to some childless couples. Cloning is yet another technological advance in science generating a lot of debate and controversy.

There are many technological advances that have become indispensable to human beings including the computer, plasma TV, CAT scan, and angioplasty.

Chemistry, physics, mathematics, earth sciences, and marine biology all affect our society, often in subtle ways. When we weigh ourselves on the scale we are using mathematics and when we convert pounds to kilograms we are using basic mathematical skills.

0006 Analyze the nature of scientific thought and inquiry.

Science is the study of phenomena that already exist in nature. Scientific investigation begins with a question or inquiry and, using the scientific method, scientists can find an answer. Because scientists are human beings, bias and prejudice in scientific investigation are potential dangers. The scientific method is designed to eliminate this bias or prejudice in our experiments. The scientific method consists of a number of steps, which when followed, yield reliable results. One step is to design an experiment by correctly manipulating the variables. The keys to a successful experiment are:

1. Controls – experimental runs with no variable manipulated; provide baseline for comparison
2. Constants – as many as possible in order to get reliable data
3. Independent variables – only a few (the fewer the number of variables the more reliable the experiment is)
4. Only one dependent variable

When we keep this in mind and design an experiment, it will be highly successful.
Any experiment must be repeated at least three times to get reliable results.
Bias, as we discussed earlier, is a big obstacle to any good research and hence must be avoided. We need to be open in our thinking and do the experiment without any preconceived ideas or notions.

0007 Understand processes for decision making related to biological problems and issues

We can make rational decisions only when we have all or most of the information about a problem. After obtaining the necessary information regarding any issue, we can make an informed decision. Let us consider cloning, which is one of the most controversial issues in science today. When accessing the value of cloning, we need to know what the real purpose of cloning is, the use of cloning a particular animal, and the relevance of cloning an animal to humanity. There are always people who object to this type of experimentation on the basis of ethics or religion. The decision making in this case is based on weighing very carefully the uses against ethical considerations. Another controversial issue is stem cell research. The use of human embryos for any purpose is always a very heated topic.

Given the advances made in information technology, it is fair to say that the public is getting more information, but it is up to the individual to make the right decision, given the fact that our religious and moral values are interrelated and play a major role in this process.

Subarea II. Cells and Cell Theory

0008 Understand cell structure and function and the cell theory.

The cell is the basic unit of all living things. There are three types of cells: prokaryotic, eukaryotic, and archaea. Archaea have some similarities with prokaryotes, but are as distantly related to prokaryotes as prokaryotes are to eukaryotes.

Prokaryotes include only bacteria and cyanobacteria (formerly known as blue-green algae). The diagram below shows the classification of prokaryotes.

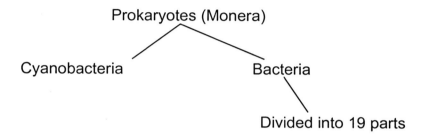

Bacterial cells have no defined nucleus or nuclear membrane. The DNA, RNA, and ribosomes float freely within the cell. The cytoplasm has a single chromosome condensed to form a **nucleoid**. Prokaryotes have a thick cell wall made up of amino sugars (glycoproteins) that provides protection, gives the cell shape, and keeps the cell from bursting. The antibiotic penicillin targets the **cell wall** of bacteria. Penicillin works by disrupting the cell wall, thus killing the cell.

The cell wall surrounds the **cell membrane** (plasma membrane). The cell membrane consists of a lipid bilayer that controls the passage of molecules in and out of the cell. Some prokaryotes have a capsule made of polysaccharides that surrounds the cell wall for extra protection.

Many bacterial cells have appendages used for movement called **flagella**. Some cells also have **pili**, which are protein strands used for attachment. Bacteria also use pili for sexual conjugation (where bacterial cells exchange DNA).

Prokaryotes are the most numerous and widespread organisms on earth. Bacteria were most likely the first cells and date back in the fossil record to 3.5 billion years. Their ability to adapt to the environment allows them to thrive in a wide variety of habitats.

Eukaryotic cells are found in protists, fungi, plants, and animals. Most eukaryotic cells are larger than prokaryotic cells. They contain many organelles, which are membrane bound areas that serve specific functions. Their cytoplasm contains a cytoskeleton which provides a protein framework for the cell. The cytoplasm also supports the organelles and contains the ions and molecules necessary for cell function. The plasma membrane contains the cytoplasm and allows molecules to pass in and out of the cell.

The membrane can bud inward to engulf outside material in a process called endocytosis. Exocytosis is a secretory mechanism, the reverse of endocytosis.

The most significant differentiation between prokaryotes and eukaryotes is that eukaryotes have a **nucleus**. The nucleus contains all of the cell's genetic information on chromosomes. The chromosomes consist of chromatin, which are complexes of DNA and proteins. The chromosomes are tightly coiled to conserve space while providing a large surface area. The nucleus is the site of transcription of the DNA into RNA.

The **nucleolus** is where ribosomes are made. There is at least one of these dark-staining bodies inside the nucleus of most eukaryotes.

The **nuclear envelope** consists of two membranes separated by a narrow space. The envelope contains many pores that let RNA out of the nucleus.

Ribosomes are the site of protein synthesis. Ribosomes may be free floating in the cytoplasm or attached to the endoplasmic reticulum. There may be up to a half a million ribosomes in a cell, depending on how much protein the cell makes.

The **endoplasmic reticulum** (ER) is folded and has a large surface area. It allows for transport of materials through and out of the cell. There are two types of ER: smooth and rough. Smooth endoplasmic reticula contain no ribosomes on their surface and are the site of lipid synthesis. Rough endoplasmic reticula have ribosomes on their surface and aid in the synthesis of proteins that are membrane bound or destined for secretion.

Many of the products made in the ER proceed to the Golgi apparatus. The **Golgi apparatus** functions to sort, modify, and package molecules that are made in the other parts of the cell (like the ER). These molecules are either sent out of the cell or to other organelles within the cell.

Lysosomes are found mainly in animal cells. These contain digestive enzymes that break down food, unnecessary substances, viruses, damaged cell components, and, eventually, the cell itself. Lysosomes may play a role in the aging process.

Mitochondria are large organelles that are the site of cellular respiration, the production of ATP that supplies energy to the cell. Muscle cells have many mitochondria because they use a great deal of energy. Mitochondria have their own DNA, RNA, and ribosomes and are capable of reproducing by binary fission if there is a great demand for additional energy. Mitochondria have two membranes: a smooth outer membrane and a folded inner membrane. The folds inside the mitochondria are called cristae. They provide a large surface area for cellular respiration.

Plastids are found only in photosynthetic organisms. They are similar to mitochondria, featuring a double membrane structure, their own DNA, RNA, and ribosomes, and the ability to reproduce. There are several types of plastids. **Chloroplasts** are the sight of photosynthesis. The stroma is the chloroplast's inner membrane space. The stroma encloses sacs called thylakoids that contain the photosynthetic pigment chlorophyll. The chlorophyll traps sunlight inside the thylakoid to generate ATP, which is used in the stroma to produce carbohydrates and other products. The **chromoplasts** make and store yellow and orange pigments that provide color to leaves, flowers, and fruits. The **amyloplasts** store starch and are food reserves. They are abundant in roots such as potatoes.

The Endosymbiotic Theory states that mitochondria and chloroplasts were once free living and possibly evolved from prokaryotic cells. At some point in our evolutionary history, they entered the eukaryotic cell and maintained a symbiotic relationship with the cell, where both the cell and organelle benefited. The fact that they both have their own DNA, RNA, ribosomes, and are capable of reproduction supports this theory.

Found only in plant cells, the **cell wall** is composed of cellulose and fibers. It is thick enough for support and protection, yet porous enough to allow water and dissolved substances to enter. **Vacuoles** are found mostly in plant cells. They hold stored food and pigments. Their large size allows them to fill with water in order to provide turgor pressure. Lack of turgor pressure causes a plant to wilt.

The **cytoskeleton**, found in both animal and plant cells, is composed of protein filaments attached to the plasma membrane and organelles. The cytoskeleton provides a framework for the cell and aids in cell movement. Three types of fibers make up the cytoskeleton:

1. **Microtubules** – The largest of the three fibers, they make up cilia and flagella for locomotion. Some examples are sperm cells, cilia that line the fallopian tubes, and tracheal cilia. Centrioles are also composed of microtubules. They aid in cell division to form the spindle fibers that pull the cell apart into two new cells. Higher plants do not have centrioles.
2. **Intermediate filaments** – Intermediate in size, they are smaller than microtubules, but larger than microfilaments. They help the cell keep its shape.

3. **Microfilaments** – Smallest of the three fibers, they are made of actin and small amounts of myosin (like in muscle tissue). They function in cell movement like cytoplasmic streaming, endocytosis, and ameboid movement. This structure pinches the two cells apart after cell division, forming two new cells.

The following is a diagram of a generalized animal cell.

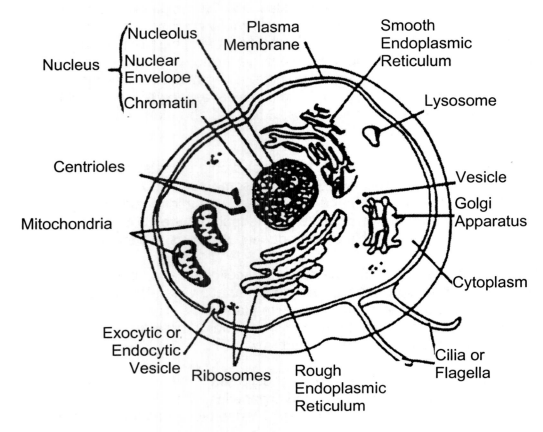

Archaea

There are three kinds of organisms with archaea cells: **methanogens**, obligate anaerobes that produce methane; **halobacteria**, which can live only in concentrated brine solutions; and **thermoacidophiles**, which can live only in acidic hot springs.

0009   Understand the chemical components of living systems and basic principles of biochemistry.

Compare and contrast hydrogen, ionic, and covalent bonds

Chemical bonds form when atoms with incomplete valence shells share or completely transfer their valence electrons. The three types of chemical bonds are covalent, ionic, and hydrogen.

Covalent bonding is the sharing of a pair of valence electrons by two atoms. A simple example of this is two hydrogen atoms. Each hydrogen atom has one valence electron in its outer shell, therefore the two hydrogen atoms come together to share their electrons. Some atoms share two pairs of valence electrons, like two oxygen atoms. This is called a double covalent bond.

The attraction for the electrons of a covalent bond is called electronegativity. The greater the electronegativity of an atom, the more it pulls the shared electrons towards itself. Electronegativity of the atoms determines whether the bond is polar or nonpolar. In **nonpolar covalent bonds**, the atoms share the electrons equally because they have the same electronegativity. This type of bonding usually occurs between two atoms of the same element. A **polar covalent bond** forms when different atoms combine, as in hydrogen and oxygen to create water. In this case, oxygen is more electronegative than hydrogen so the oxygen pulls the hydrogen electrons toward itself.

Ionic bonds form when one atom strips away one electron from another atom. An example an ionic bond is sodium chloride (NaCl). A single electron in the outer shell of sodium joins the chloride atom with seven electrons in its outer shell. The sodium atom now has a +1 charge and the chloride atom has a -1 charge. The charges attract each other to form an ionic bond. Ionic compounds are called salts.   In a dry salt crystal, the bond is so strong it requires a great deal of strength to break it apart. But, place the salt crystal in water, and the bond dissolves easily as the attraction between the two atoms decreases.

The weakest of the three bonds is the **hydrogen bond**. A hydrogen bond forms when one electronegative atom shares a hydrogen atom with another electronegative atom. An example of a hydrogen bond is a water molecule (H_2O) bonding with an ammonia molecule (NH_3). The H^+ atom of the water molecule attracts the negatively charged nitrogen in a weak bond. Weak hydrogen bonds are beneficial because they can briefly form, the atoms can respond to one another, and then break apart allowing formation of new bonds. Hydrogen bonding plays a very important role in the chemistry of life.

Analyze the structure and function of carbohydrates, lipids, and proteins

A compound consists of two or more elements. There are four major chemical compounds found in the cells and bodies of living things: carbohydrates, lipids, proteins, and nucleic acids.

Monomers are the simplest unit of structure. **Monomers** combine to form **polymers**, or long chains, making a large variety of molecules. Monomers combine through the process of condensation reactions (also called dehydration synthesis). In this process, one molecule of water is removed between each of the adjoining molecules. In order to break the molecules apart in a polymer, water molecules are added between monomers, thus breaking the bonds between them. This process is called hydrolysis.

Carbohydrates contain a ratio of two hydrogen atoms for each carbon and oxygen $(CH_2O)_n$. Carbohydrates include sugars and starches. They provide energy for cellular function. **Monosaccharides** are the simplest sugars and include glucose, fructose, and galactose. They are major nutrients for cells. In cellular respiration, the cells extract the energy from glucose molecules. **Disaccharides** are made by joining two monosaccharides by condensation to form a glycosidic linkage (covalent bond between two monosaccharides). Maltose is the combination of two glucose molecules, lactose is the combination of glucose and galactose, and sucrose is the combination of glucose and fructose.

Polysaccharides consist of many monomers joined together. They are storage material hydrolyzed as needed to provide sugar for cells or building material for structures protecting the cell. Examples of polysaccharides include starch, glycogen, cellulose, and chitin.

> **Starch** is a major energy storage molecule in plants consisting of glucose monomers.
>
> **Glycogen** is a major energy storage molecule in animals consisting of many glucose molecules.
>
> **Cellulose** is a component of plant cell walls, its function is structural. Many animals lack the enzymes necessary to hydrolyze cellulose, so it simply adds bulk (fiber) to the diet.
>
> **Chitin** is a component of the exoskeleton of arthropods and fungi. Chitin contains an amino sugar (glycoprotein).

Lipids consists of glycerol (an alcohol) and three fatty acids. Lipids are **hydrophobic** (water fearing) and will not mix with water. There are three important families of lipids: fats, phospholipids, and steroids.

Fats consist of glycerol (alcohol) and three fatty acids. Fatty acids are long carbon skeletons. The nonpolar carbon-hydrogen bonds in the tails of fatty acids are highly hydrophobic. Saturated fats are solids at room temperature and come from animal sources (e.g., butter and lard). Unsaturated fats are liquid at room temperature and come from plants (e.g., soy, peanut, canola).

Phospholipids are vital components of cell membranes. In a phospholipid, a phosphate group linked to a nitrogen group replaces one or two fatty acids. Phopholipids consist of a **polar** (charged) head that is hydrophilic (water loving) and a **nonpolar** (uncharged) tail which is hydrophobic. This allows the membrane to orient itself with the polar heads facing the interstitial fluid found outside the cell and the nonpolar tails facing the internal fluid of the cell.

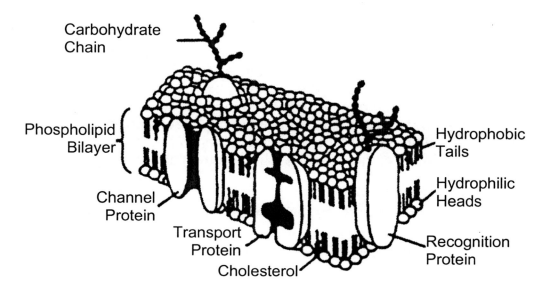

Steroids are insoluble and are composed of a carbon skeleton consisting of four inter-connected rings. An important steroid is cholesterol, which is the precursor from which other steroids are synthesized. Hormones, including cortisone, testosterone, estrogen, and progesterone, are steroids. Their insolubility keeps them from dissolving in body fluids.

Proteins account for about fifty percent of the dry weight of animals and bacteria. Proteins function in structure and support (e.g., connective tissue, hair, feathers, and quills), storage of amino acids (e.g., albumin in eggs and casein in milk), transport of substances (e.g. hemoglobin), coordination of body activities (e.g. insulin), signal transduction (e.g. membrane receptor proteins), contraction (e.g., muscles, cilia, and flagella), body defense (e.g. antibodies), and as enzymes to speed up chemical reactions.

All proteins consist of different arrangements of twenty **amino acids**. An analogy can be drawn between the twenty amino acids and the alphabet. We can form millions of words using an alphabet of only twenty-six letters. Similarly, organisms can create many different proteins using the twenty amino acids. This results in the formation of many different proteins. An amino acid contains an amino group, an acid group, and a radical group that varies and defines the amino acid. Proteins form through condensation reactions between amino acids. The bond formed between two amino acids is called a peptide bond. Polymers of amino acids are called polypeptide chains.

There are four levels of protein structure: primary, secondary, tertiary, and quaternary.

Primary structure is the protein's unique sequence of amino acids. A slight change in primary structure can affect a protein's conformation and its ability to function. **Secondary structure** is the coils and folds of polypeptide chains. The coils and folds are the result of hydrogen bonds along the polypeptide backbone. The secondary structure is either in the form of an alpha helix or a pleated sheet. The alpha helix is a coil held together by hydrogen bonds. A pleated sheet is the polypeptide chain folding back and forth. **Tertiary structure** is formed by bonding between the side chains of the amino acids. For example, disulfide bridges form when two sulfhydryl groups on the amino acids bond together to form a strong covalent bond. **Quaternary structure** is the overall structure of a protein resulting from the interaction of two or more polypeptide chains. An example of this is hemoglobin. Hemoglobin consists of two kinds of polypeptide chains.

Analyze the properties of water and its significance to living organisms

Water is necessary for life. The molecular structure of water accounts for its unique properties. Water is a polar substance. This means it is formed by covalent bonds that make it electrically lopsided.

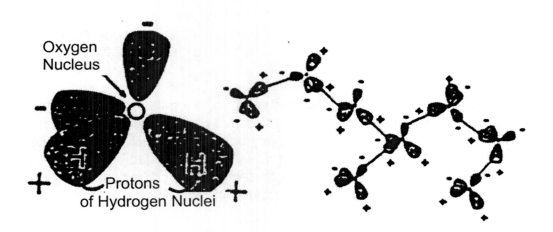

Oxygen
Nucleus

Protons
of Hydrogen Nuclei

A water molecule showing polarity   Hydrogen bonding between
created by covalent bonds   water molecules

BIOLOGY   22

Water molecules are attracted to other water molecules due to this electrical imbalance and this attraction allows for two important properties: adhesion and cohesion. Adhesion is when water sticks to other substances like the xylem of a stem, aiding the water in traveling up the stem to the leaves.

Cohesion is the ability of water molecules to stick to each other by hydrogen bonding. This allows for surface tension on a body of water, or capillarity, which allows water to move through vessels. Surface tension is how difficult it is to stretch or break the surface of a liquid. Cohesion allows water to move against gravity.

Several other important properties of water include:

- Water is a good solvent. An aqueous solution is one in which water is the solvent. It provides a medium for chemical reactions to occur.
- Water has a high specific heat of 1 calorie per gram per degree Celsius, allowing it to cool and warm slowly and allowing organisms to adapt to temperature changes. Water has a high boiling point; thus, it is a good coolant.
- Water's ability to evaporate stabilizes the environment and allows organisms to maintain body temperature.
- Water has a high freezing point and a lower density as a solid than as a liquid. Water is most dense at four degrees celsius. This allows ice to float on top of water so a whole body of water does not freeze during the winter. Because of this property of water, aquatic animals can survive the winter.

Understand pH chemistry in biological systems

The pH scale measures how acidic or basic a solution is. An acid is a solution that increases the hydrogen ion concentration of a solution. An example is hydrochloric acid (HCl). A base is a solution that reduces the hydrogen ion concentration. An example is sodium hydroxide (NaOH).

	pH	Hydrogen Ion Concentration
Acid	0 – 6.9	Increases
Base	7.1 – 14.0	Decreases

The pH scale ranges from zero to fourteen. Seven is a neutral solution and is the pH of pure water. A pH between zero and 6.9 is acidic. Stomach acid has a pH of 2.0. A pH between 7.1 and 14 is basic. Common household bleach has a pH of 12.

The internal pH of most living organisms is close to 7. Human blood has a pH of 7.4. Variation from this neutral pH can be harmful to the organism. Biological fluids resist pH variation due to buffers that minimize the effects of H^+ and OH^- concentrations. A buffer accepts or donates H+ ions from or to the solution when they are in excess or depleted.

The pH of a substance has a dramatic effect on the environment as well. Acids greatly affect the environment. Acidic precipitation is rain, snow, or fog with a pH less than 5.6.

Sulfur oxides and nitrogen oxides in the environment that react with water in the air cause acidic precipitation. A change in pH in the environment can affect the solubility of minerals in the soil, which can delay forest growth.

0010 Analyze physiological processes of cells.

Cells are dynamic entities that carry out a number of important physiological processes. Here we discuss cellular processes including transport and energy production.

Understand the importance of active and passive transport

Cell transport is necessary to maintain homeostasis, or balance between the cell and its external environment. Cell membranes are selectively permeable, which is the key to transport. Not all molecules may pass through easily. Some molecules require energy or carrier molecules and may only cross when needed.

In order to understand cellular transport, it is important to understand the structure of the cell membrane. All organisms contain cell membranes that regulate the flow of materials into and out of the cell. The current model for the cell membrane is the Fluid Mosaic Model, which describes the ability of lipids and proteins to move and change places, giving the membrane fluidity.

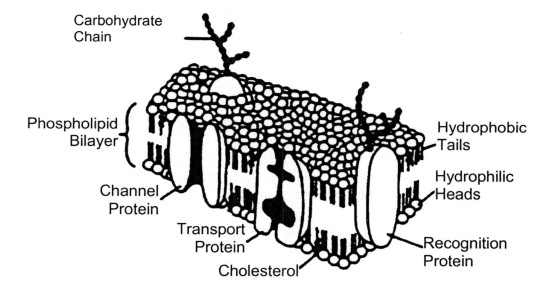

Cell membranes have the following characteristics:

1.   They are made of phospholipids, which have polar, charged heads with a hydrophilic (water loving) phosphate group and two nonpolar, hydrophobic (water fearing) lipid tails. Membranes orient themselves with the polar heads facing the fluid inside and outside the cell and the hydrophobic lipid tails sandwiched in between.

2.   They contain embedded proteins (integral proteins) and proteins on the surface (peripheral proteins). These proteins may act as channels for transport, contain enzymes, act as receptor sites, act to stick cells together, or attach to the cytoskeleton to give the cell shape.

3.   They contain cholesterol, which alters the fluidity of the membrane.

4.   They contain oligosaccharides (small carbohydrate polymers) on the outside of the membrane. These act as markers that help distinguish one cell from another.

5.   They contain receptors made of glycoproteins that can attach to certain molecules such as hormones.

Passive transport does not require energy and moves substances with the concentration gradient (high to low). Small molecules may pass through the membrane in this manner. Two examples of passive transport are diffusion and osmosis. **Diffusion** is the movement of molecules from areas of high concentration to areas of low concentration. It normally involves small uncharged particles like oxygen. **Osmosis** is the diffusion of water across a semi-permeable membrane. Osmosis may cause cells to swell or shrink, depending on the internal and external environments. The following terms describe the relationship of the cell to the environment.

   Isotonic - Water concentration is equal inside and outside the cell. Net movement in either direction is equal.

   Hypertonic - "Hyper" refers to the amount of dissolved particles. The more particles in a solution, the lower its water concentration. Therefore, when a cell is hypertonic to its environment, there is more water outside the cell than inside. Water will move into the cell and the cell will swell. If the environment is hypertonic to the cell, there is more water inside the cell. Water will move out of the cell and the cell will shrink.

   Hypotonic - "Hypo" again refers to the amount of dissolved particles. The fewer particles in solution, the higher its water concentration. When a cell is hypotonic to its environment, there is more water inside the cell than outside. Water will move out of the cell and the cell will shrink. If the environment is hypotonic to the cell, there is more water outside the cell than inside. Water will move into the cell and the cell will swell.

The **facilitated diffusion** mechanism does not require energy, but does require a carrier protein. An example is glucose transport, which requires insulin.

Active transport requires energy. ATP or an electrical charge difference supplies the energy. Active transport may move materials either with or against a concentration gradient. Some examples of active transport are:

> **Sodium-Potassium Pump** - maintains an electrical difference across the cell membrane. This is useful in restoring ion balance so nerves can continue to function. It exchanges sodium ions for potassium ions across the plasma membrane in animal cells.

> **Stomach Acid Pump** - exports hydrogen ions to lower the pH of the stomach and increase acidity.

> **Calcium Pumps** - actively pump calcium outside of the cell and are important in nerve and muscle transmission.

Active transport involves a membrane potential, which is a charge on the membrane. The charge works like a magnet and may cause transport proteins to alter their shape, thus allowing substances in or out of the cell.

The transport of large molecules depends on the fluidity of the membrane, which cholesterol in the membrane controls. **Exocytosis** is the release of large particles by vesicles fusing with the plasma membrane. In **endocytosis**, the cell takes in macromolecules and particulate matter by forming vesicles derived from the plasma membrane. There are three types of endocytosis in animal cells. **Phagocytosis** is when a particle is engulfed by pseudopodia and packaged in a vacuole. In **pinocytosis**, the cell takes in extracellular fluid in small vesicles. **Receptor-mediated endocytosis** is when the membrane vesicles bud inward to allow a cell to take in large amounts of certain substances. The vesicles have proteins with receptors that are specific for the substance.

Analyze the structure and function of enzymes and factors

Enzymes are biological catalysts that speed up reactions. Enzymes are the most diverse of all proteins. They are not used up in a reaction and are recyclable. Each enzyme is specific for a single reaction. Enzymes act on a substrate. The substrate is the material to be broken down or put back together. Most enzymes end in the suffix -ase (lipase, amylase). The prefix is the substrate being acted on (lipids, sugars).

$$\text{Substrate} \xrightarrow{\text{Enzyme}} \text{Product}$$

The active site is the region of the enzyme that binds to the substrate. There are two theories for how the active site functions. The **lock and key theory** states that the shape of the enzyme is specific because it fits into the substrate like a key fits into a lock. The enzyme aids in holding molecules close together so reactions can easily occur. The **induced fit theory** states that an enzyme can stretch and bend to fit the substrate. This is the most accepted theory.

Many factors can affect enzyme activity. Temperature and pH are two such factors. High and low temperatures can inactivate or inhibit enzymes. The optimal pH for most enzymes is between 6 and 8, with a few exceptions.

Cofactors aid in enzyme function. Cofactors may be inorganic or organic. Organic cofactors are coenzymes. Vitamins are examples of coenzymes. Some chemicals can inhibit an enzyme's function. **Competitive inhibitors** occupy the enzyme active site and prevent the substrate from binding. **Noncompetitive inhibitors** bind the enzyme in a location other than the active site, but still interrupt substrate binding. In most cases, noncompetitive inhibitors alter the shape of the enzyme. An **allosteric enzyme** can exist in two shapes, they are active in one form and inactive in the other.

Understand the significance of photosynthesis and respiration to living organisms

Respiration is the metabolic pathway by which cells break down food (i.e. glucose) to produce energy in the form of ATP. Both plants and animals utilize respiration to create energy. In respiration, energy is released by the transfer of electrons in **oxidation-reduction (redox)** reactions. The oxidation phase of this reaction is the loss of an electron and the reduction phase is the gain of an electron. Redox reactions are important in all stages of respiration.

Glycolysis is the first step in respiration. It occurs in the cytoplasm of the cell and does not require oxygen. Specific enzymes catalyze each of the ten stages of glycolysis. The following is a summary of these stages.

In the first stage the reactant is glucose. For energy to be released from glucose, it must be converted to a reactive compound. This conversion occurs through the phosphorylation of a molecule of glucose by the use of two molecules of ATP. This is an investment of energy by the cell. The 6-carbon product, called fructose -1,6-bisphosphate, breaks into two 3-carbon molecules of sugar. A phosphate group is added to each sugar molecule and hydrogen atoms are removed. Hydrogen is picked up by NAD^+ (a vitamin). Since there are two sugar molecules, two molecules of NADH are formed. The reduction (addition of hydrogen) of NAD^+ allows the potential for energy transfer.

As the phosphate bonds are broken, ATP is produced. Two ATP molecules are generated as each original 3-carbon sugar molecule is converted to pyruvic acid (pyruvate). A total of four ATP molecules are made in the four stages. Since two molecules of ATP were needed to start the reaction in stage 1, there is a net gain of two ATP molecules at the end of glycolysis. This accounts for only two percent of the total energy in a molecule of glucose.

Pyruvate, the end product of glycolysis, undergoes the following alterations before entering the **Krebs cycle**. Conversion to acetyl-CoA (coenzyme A), a 2-carbon acetyl group formed when a 3-carbon pyruvic acid molecule loses one molecule of carbon dioxide (CO_2) the loss of a hydrogen to NAD^+ (reduced to NADH). Acetyl CoA then enters the Krebs cycle. For each molecule of glucose, two molecules of Acetyl CoA enter the Krebs cycle (one for each molecule of pyruvic acid formed in glycolysis).

The **Krebs cycle** (or citric acid cycle) occurs in four major steps. First, the 2-carbon acetyl CoA combines with a 4-carbon molecule to form a 6-carbon citric acid molecule. Next, two carbons are lost as carbon dioxide (CO_2) and a 4-carbon molecule forms and becomes available to join with CoA to form citric acid again. Since we started with two molecules of CoA, two turns of the Krebs cycle are necessary to process the original molecule of glucose. In the third step, eight hydrogen atoms are released and picked up by FAD and NAD (vitamins and electron carriers). Finally, for each molecule of CoA (remember there were two to start with) you get:

> 3 molecules of NADH x 2 cycles
> 1 molecule of $FADH_2$ x 2 cycles
> 1 molecule of ATP x 2 cycles

At this point, the cell has made a total of four molecules of ATP, two from glycolysis and one from each of the two turns of the Krebs cycle. The cell has released six molecules of carbon dioxide, two prior to entering the Krebs cycle and two for each of the two turns of the Krebs cycle. The cell has made twelve carrier molecules, ten NADH and two $FADH_2$. These carrier molecules carry electrons to the electron transport chain.

The Krebs cycle produces ATP by substrate level phosphorylation. Notice that the Krebs cycle does not produce much ATP, but functions mostly in the transfer of electrons for use in the electron transport chain that produces the most ATP for the cell.

In the **Electron Transport Chain,** NADH transfers electrons from glycolysis and the Krebs cycle to the first molecule in the chain of molecules embedded in the inner membrane of the mitochondrion.

Most of the molecules in the electron transport chain are proteins. Nonprotein molecules are also part of the chain and are essential for the catalytic functions of certain enzymes. The electron transport chain does not make ATP directly. Instead, it breaks up a large free energy drop into more manageable ones. The chain uses electrons to pump H^+ ions across the mitochondrial membrane. The H^+ gradient drives ATP synthesis in a process called **chemiosmosis** (oxidative phosphorylation). ATP synthetase and energy generated by the movement of hydrogen ions coming off of NADH and $FADH_2$ builds ATP from ADP on the inner membrane of the mitochondrion. Each NADH yields three molecules of ATP (10 x 3) and each $FADH_2$ yields two molecules of ATP (2 x 2). The electron transport chain and oxidative phosphorylation produces 34 ATP.

Thus, the net gain from the whole process of respiration is 36 molecules of ATP:

Glycolysis – 4 ATP made, 2 ATP spent = net gain of 2 ATP
Acetyl CoA – 2 ATP spent
Krebs cycle – 1 ATP made for each turn of the cycle = net gain of 2 ATP
Electron transport chain – 34 ATP gained

Photosynthesis is an anabolic process that stores energy in the form of a three carbon sugar. We will use glucose as an example for this section.

The formula for photosynthesis is:
$$CO_2 + H_2O + \text{energy (from sunlight)} \rightarrow C_6H_{12}O_6 + O_2$$

Photosynthesis occurs only in organisms that contain chloroplasts (i.e., plants, some bacteria, and some protists). There are a few terms we need to understand before discussing photosynthesis.

An **autotroph** (self-feeder) is an organism that makes its own food from the energy of the sun or other elements. Autotrophs include:

1. **photoautotrophs** - make food from light and carbon dioxide releasing oxygen for respiration.
2. **chemoautotrophs** - oxidize sulfur and ammonia. Some bacteria are chemoautotrophs.

Heterotrophs (other feeder) are organisms that must eat other living things to obtain energy. Another term for heterotrophs is **consumers**. All animals are heterotrophs.

Decomposers (or saprotrophs) break down dead organisms. Bacteria and fungi are examples of decomposers.

Chloroplasts are the site of photosynthesis. Similar to mitochondria, chloroplasts have an increased surface area (thylakoid membrane). Chloroplasts also contain a fluid called stroma between the stacks of thylakoids. The thylakoid membrane contains pigments (chlorophyll) that capture light energy.

Photosynthesis reverses the electron flow. Chloroplasts split water into hydrogen and oxygen. The oxygen is a waste product in the reduction of carbon dioxide to sugar (glucose). This requires the input of solar energy.

Photosynthesis occurs in two stages, the light reactions and the dark reactions (Calvin cycle). The conversion of solar energy to chemical energy occurs in the light reactions. The absorption of light by chlorophyll initiates electron transfer, which causes water to split, releasing oxygen as a waste product. The chemical energy created in the light reaction is in the form of NADPH. ATP is also produced by a process called photophosphorylation.

The second stage of photosynthesis is the **Calvin cycle**. Carbon dioxide in the air is incorporated into organic molecules already in the chloroplast. The NADPH produced in the light reaction is used as reducing power for the reduction of the carbon to carbohydrate. ATP from the light reaction is also needed to convert carbon dioxide to carbohydrate (sugar).

Solar energy facilitates the process of photosynthesis. Visible light ranges in wavelengths of 750 nanometers (red light) to 380 nanometers (violet light). As a wavelength decreases, the amount of energy available increases. Light is carried as photons, which are fixed quantities of energy. Light is reflected (what we see), transmitted, or absorbed (what the plant uses). Plant pigments capture light of specific wavelengths. Remember that we see the reflected light as color. Plant pigments include:

> Chlorophyll *a* – reflects green/blue light, absorbs red light
> Chlorophyll *b* – reflects yellow/green light, absorbs red light
> Carotenoids – reflects yellow/orange light, absorbs violet/blue light

The pigments absorb photons. The energy from the light excites electrons in the chlorophyll that jump to orbitals with more potential energy and reach an "excited" or unstable state.

Primary electron acceptors trap the high energy electrons located on the thylakoid membrane. The electron acceptors and pigments form reaction centers called photosystems that are capable of capturing light energy. Photosystems contain a reaction-center chlorophyll that releases an electron to the primary electron acceptor. This transfer is the first step of the light reactions. There are two photosystems, named according to their date of discovery, not their order of occurrence.

Photosystem I consists of a pair of chlorophyll *a* molecules. Photosystem I is also called P700 because it absorbs light of 700 nanometers. Photosystem I makes ATP whose energy is necessary for to glucose synthesis.

Photosystem II is also called P680 because it absorbs light of 680 nanometers. Photosystem II produces ATP + NADPH$_2$ and the waste gas oxygen.

Both photosystems are bound to the **thylakoid membrane**, close to the electron acceptors.

The production of ATP is termed **photophosphorylation** due to the use of light. Photosystem I uses cyclic photophosphorylation because the pathway occurs in a cycle. It can also use noncyclic photophosphorylation which starts with light and ends with glucose. Photosystem II uses noncyclic photophosphorylation only.

Below is a diagram of the relationship between cellular respiration and photosynthesis.

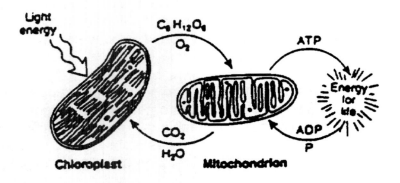

Compare aerobic and anaerobic respiration

Glycolysis generates ATP with oxygen (aerobic) or without oxygen (anaerobic). We have already discussed aerobic respiration. Anaerobic respiration is also known as fermentation. Fermentation generates ATP by substrate level phosphorylation if there is enough NAD$^+$ present to accept electrons during oxidation. In anaerobic respiration, NAD$^+$ is regenerated by transferring electrons to pyruvate. There are two common types of fermentation.

In **alcoholic fermentation**, pyruvate is converted to ethanol in two steps. In the first step, carbon dioxide is released from the pyruvate. In the second step, ethanol is produced by the reduction of acetaldehyde by NADH. This results in the regeneration of NAD$^+$ for glycolysis. Yeast and some bacteria carry out alcoholic fermentation. NADH reduces pyruvate to form lactate as a waste product in the process of **lactic acid fermentation**. Animal cells and some bacteria that do not use oxygen utilize lactic acid fermentation to make ATP. Lactic acid forms when pyruvic acid accepts hydrogen from NADH. A buildup of lactic acid is what causes muscle soreness following exercise.

Energy remains stored in the lactic acid or alcohol until needed. This is not an efficient type of respiration. When oxygen is present, aerobic respiration occurs after glycolysis.

Both aerobic and anaerobic pathways oxidize glucose to pyruvate by glycolysis and both pathways have NAD^+ as the oxidizing agent. A substantial difference between the two pathways is that in fermentation an organic molecule such as pyruvate or acetaldehyde is the final electron acceptor. In respiration, the final electron acceptor is oxygen. Another key difference is that respiration yields much more energy from a sugar molecule than does fermentation. Respiration can produce up to 18 times more ATP than fermentation.

0011   Analyze cell growth, division, and differentiation

Knowledge of cell division

The purpose of cell division is growth and repair in body (somatic) cells and replenishment or creation of sex cells for reproduction. There are two forms of cell division: mitosis and meiosis. **Mitosis** is the division of somatic cells and **meiosis** is the division of sex cells (eggs and sperm).

Mitosis has two parts: the **mitotic (M) phase** and **interphase.** In the mitotic phase, mitosis and cytokinesis divide the nucleus and cytoplasm, respectively. This phase is the shortest phase of the cell cycle. Interphase is the stage where the cell grows and copies the chromosomes in preparation for the mitotic phase. Interphase occurs in three stages of growth: the **G1** (growth) period, when the cell grows and metabolizes; the **S** (synthesis) period, when the cell makes new DNA; and the **G2** (growth) period, when the cell makes new proteins and organelles in preparation for cell division.

The mitotic phase is a continuum of change, although we divide it into five distinct stages: prophase, prometaphase, metaphase, anaphase, and telophase.

Prophase
1. Chromatin condenses forming visible chromosomes
2. The nucleolus disappears and the nuclear membrane breaks apart
3. Mitotic spindles composed of microtubules form that will eventually pull the chromosomes apart
4. The cytoskeleton breaks down and the action of centrioles push the spindles to the poles or opposite ends of the cell

Prometaphase
1. The nuclear membrane fragments and allows the spindle microtubules to interact with the chromosomes
2. Kinetochore fibers attach to the chromosomes at the centromere region.

Metaphase
1. Begins when the centrosomes are at opposite ends of the cell
2. The centromeres of all the chromosomes align with one another

Anaphase
1. The centromeres split in half and homologous chromosomes separate
2. The chromosomes are pulled to the poles of the cell, with identical sets at either end

Telophase
1. Two nuclei form with a full set of DNA that is identical to the parent cell
2. The nucleoli become visible and the nuclear membrane reassembles
3. A cell plate forms in plant cells and a cleavage furrow forms in animal cells. The cell pinches into two cells
4. Cytokinesis, or division of the cytoplasm and organelles, occurs

Below is a diagram of mitosis.

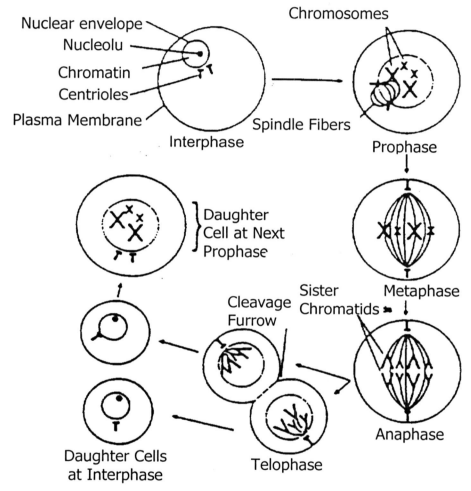

Mitosis in an Animal Cell

Meiosis is similar to mitosis, but there are two consecutive cell divisions, meiosis I and meiosis II, which reduce the chromosome number by one half. This way, when the sperm and egg join during fertilization, the two haploid cells produce a diploid zygote.

Similar to mitosis, meiosis is preceded by an interphase during which the chromosome replicates. The steps of meiosis are:

Prophase I

- The replicated chromosomes condense and pair with homologues in a process called synapsis (this forms a tetrad)
- Crossing over, the exchange of genetic material between homologues to further increase diversity, occurs during prophase I

Metaphase I

- The homologous pairs attach to spindle fibers after lining up in the middle of the cell

Anaphase I

- The sister chromatids remain joined and move to the poles of the cell.

Telophase I

- The homologous chromosome pairs continue to separate
- Each pole now has a haploid chromosome set.
- Telophase I occurs simultaneously with cytokinesis
- In animal cells, a cleavage furrow forms and, in plant cells, a cell plate appears

Prophase II

- A spindle apparatus forms and the chromosomes condense.

Metaphase II

- Sister chromatids line up in center of cell
- The centromeres divide and the sister chromatids begin to separate

Anaphase II

- The separated chromosomes move to opposite ends of the cell.

Telophase II

- Cytokinesis occurs, resulting in four haploid daughter cells.

Below is a diagram of meiosis.

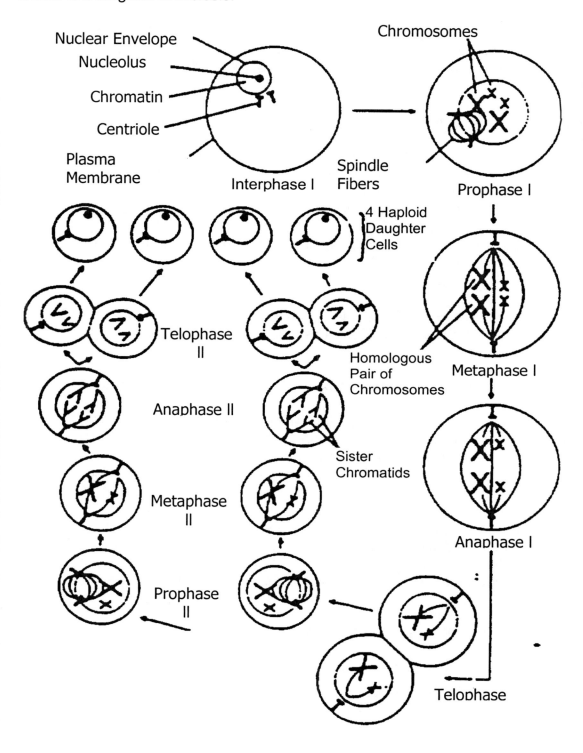

Understand genetic diversity

Meiosis and fertilization are responsible for genetic diversity. There are several mechanisms that contribute to genetic variation in sexual reproductive organisms. Three of them are independent assortment of chromosomes, crossing over, and random fertilization.

At the metaphase I stage of meiosis, each homologous pair of chromosomes sits along the metaphase plate. The orientation of the homologous pairs is random and independent of the other pairs. This results in an **independent assortment** of maternal and paternal chromosomes. Based on this information, it seems as though each chromosome in a gamete would be of only maternal or paternal origin. A process called crossing over prevents this from happening.

Crossing over occurs during prophase I. At this point, nonsister chromatids cross and exchange corresponding segments. Crossing over results in the combination of DNA from both parents, allowing for greater genetic variation in sexual life cycles.

Random fertilization also results in genetic variation. Each parent has about 8 million possible chromosome combinations. This allows for over 60 trillion diploid combinations.

Understand the relationship between an unrestricted cell cycle and cancer

The restriction point in the cell cycle occurs late in the G_1 phase of the cell cycle. If all the internal and external cell systems are working properly, the cell proceeds to replicate. Cells may also decide not to proceed past the restriction point. This nondividing cell state is called the G_0 phase. Many specialized cells remain in this state.

The density of cells also regulates cell division. Density-dependent inhibition is when the cells crowd one another and consume all the nutrients, therefore halting cell division. Cancer cells do not respond to density-dependent inhibition. They divide excessively and invade other tissues. As long as there are nutrients, cancer cells are "immortal."

Analyze the role of stem cells in cellular differentiation

Differentiation is the process in which cells become specialized in structure and function. The fate of the cell is usually maintained through many subsequent generations. Gene regulatory proteins can generate many cell types during development. Scientists believe that these proteins are passed down to the next generation of cells to ensure the specialized expression of the genes.

Stem cells are not terminally differentiated. They can divide for as long as the animal is alive. When the stem cell divides, its daughter cells can either remain a stem cell or proceed with terminal differentiation. There are many types of stem cells that are specialized for different classes of terminally differentiated cells.

Embryonic stem cells give rise to all the tissues and cell types in the body. In culture, these cells have led to the creation of animal tissue that can replace damaged tissues. The hope is that with continued research scientists will be able to culture embryonic stem cells to replace damaged muscles, tissues, and organs.

Subarea III. Characteristics of Organisms

0012 Understand the principles of taxonomy and classification in biology

Knowledge of the classification of organisms

Scientists estimate that there are more than ten million different species of living things. Of these, 1.5 million have been named and classified. Systems of classification delineate similarities between organisms and provide scientists with a worldwide system of organization.

Carolus Linnaeus is termed the father of taxonomy. **Taxonomy** is the science of classification. Linnaeus based his system on morphology (study of structure). Later, scientists also used evolutionary relationships (phylogeny) to sort and group species. The modern classification system uses binomial nomenclature, a two-word name for every species. The genus is the first part of the name and the species is the second part. Notice in the levels explained below that *Homo sapiens* is the scientific name for humans. Starting with the kingdom, the groups get smaller and more alike as one moves down the levels in the classification of humans:

Kingdom: Animalia, Phylum: Chordata, Subphylum: Vertebrata, Class: Mammalia, Order: Primate, Family: Hominidae, Genus: Homo, Species: sapiens

Members of a species are able to reproduce successfully with other members of their species.

Several different morphological criteria are used to classify organisms:

1. **Ancestral characters** - characteristics that are unchanged after evolution (e.g. 5 digits on the hand of an ape).
2. **Derived characters** - characteristics that have evolved more recently (e.g. the absence of a tail on an ape).
3. **Conservative characters** - traits that change slowly.
4. **Homologous characters** - characteristics with the same genetic basis but used for a different function. (e.g., wing of a bat, arm of a human. The bone structure is the same, but the limbs are used for different purposes).
5. **Analogous characters** – structures that differ, but used for similar purposes (e.g. the wing of a bird and the wing of a butterfly).
6. **Convergent evolution** - development of similar adaptations by organisms that are unrelated.

Biological characteristics are also used to classify organisms. Protein comparison, DNA comparison, and analysis of fossilized DNA are powerful comparative methods used to measure evolutionary relationships between species. Taxonomists consider the organism's life history, biochemical (DNA) makeup, behavior, and geographical distribution. The fossil record can also reveal evolutionary relationships.

Analyzing a phylogenetic tree or cladogram of related species

The typical graphic product of a classification is a **phylogenetic tree**, which represents a hypothesis of the relationships based on branching of lineages through time within a group.

Every time you see a phylogenetic tree, you should be aware that it is making statements on the degree of similarity between organisms, or the particular pattern in which the various lineages diverged (phylogenetic history).

Cladistics is the study of phylogenetic relationships of organisms by analysis of shared, derived character states. Cladograms show evolutionary pathways. Character states are polarized in cladistic analysis to be plesiomorphous (ancestral features), symplesiomorphous (shared ancestral features), apomorphous (derived features), and synapomorphous (shared, derived features).

Analyzing the impact of evolution and modern genetics in the classification system

The current five-kingdom system separates prokaryotes from eukaryotes. The prokaryotes belong to the Kingdom Monera while the eukaryotes belong to Kingdoms Protista, Plantae, Fungi, and Animalia. Recent comparisons of nucleic acids and proteins between different groups of organisms have revealed problems in the five-kingdom system. Based on these comparisons, alternative kingdom systems have emerged. Scientists have proposed six and eight kingdom systems as well as a three-domain system as more accurate. It is important to note that classification systems evolve as more information regarding characteristics and evolutionary histories of organisms arise.

0013   Analyze reproduction, development, and life cycles of living organisms

Life has defining properties. Some of the more important processes and properties associated with life include:

- Order – an organism's complex organization
- Reproduction – life only comes from life (biogenesis)
- Energy utilization – organisms use and convert energy to do many kinds of work
- Growth and development – DNA directed growth and development
- Adaptation to the environment – occurs by homeostasis (ability to maintain a certain status), response to stimuli, and evolution

Recognize the levels of organization

Life is highly organized. The organization of living systems builds on levels from small to increasingly larger and more complex. All aspects, whether it is a cell or an ecosystem, have the same requirements to sustain life. Life is organized from simple to complex in the following way:

Atoms → molecules → organelles → cells → tissues → organs → organ systems→organism

Recognize the different classifications of living organisms and their reproductive characteristics

Although **viruses** are not classified as living things, they greatly affect other living things by disrupting cell activity. Viruses are obligate parasites because they rely on the host for their own reproduction. Viruses consist of a protein coat and a nucleic acid, either DNA or RNA. A bacteriophage is a virus that infects a bacterium. Animal viruses are classified by the type of nucleic acid, presence of RNA replicase, and presence of a protein coat.

There are two types of viral reproductive cycles:

1.   **Lytic cycle** - The virus enters the host cell and makes copies of its nucleic acids and protein coats and reassembles. It then lyses or breaks out of the host cell and infects other nearby cells, repeating the process.
2.   **Lysogenic cycle** - The virus may remain dormant within the cell until some factor activates it and stimulates it to break out of the cell. Herpes is an example of a lysogenic virus.

Member of the Kingdom Monera are single-celled organisms that do not have a nucleus, but have nuclear material inside the cells. This group consists of bacteria and blue-green bacteria, which exist as uni- or multicellular organisms.

Blue-green bacteria are small one-celled organisms that are photosynthetic. Bacteria reproduce asexually (from a single parent) by fission, in which one organism divides into two. The chromosome of the bacterial cell, which is circular, makes a copy of itself and then the cell divides resulting in two identical cells. If the conditions for asexual reproduction are ideal, a bacterium can reproduce in about 20 minutes. All new organisms are exact clones of the parent.

Protists are larger than bacteria and are of three types – animal like, plant like and fungus like. Animal-like protists reproduce asexually by fission (by dividing into two) and spores. Spores are special cells that develop into new organisms.

Plant-like protists reproduce by fission, spores, and by gametes and conjugation, which is somewhat similar to sexual reproduction. Fungus-like protists form spores and reproduce.

Mushrooms, molds, mildews, yeasts, rusts, and smuts are all members of the Kingdom Fungi. Fungi are of three kinds – sporangium fungi, club fungi, and sac fungi. Sporangium fungi (molds) reproduce by forming spores in sporangia, which are specialized structures that produce spores. Club fungi (mushrooms) reproduce by spores, which are produced in club-shaped structures within the gills. These gills are located in the cap of the fungi. Sac fungi (yeasts) reproduce by budding (parent cell forming a bud, which ultimately breaks) and spores produced in the sacs.

Plants accomplish reproduction through alternation of generations. Simply stated, a haploid stage in the plants life history alternates with a diploid stage. The diploid sporophyte divides by meiosis to reduce the chromosome number to the haploid gametophyte generation. The haploid gametophytes undergo mitosis to produce gametes (sperm and eggs). Finally, the haploid gametes combine to return to the diploid sporophyte stage.

The non-vascular plants need water to reproduce. The vascular, non-seeded plants reproduce with spores and also need water to reproduce. Gymnosperms use seeds for reproduction and do not require water.

Angiosperms are the most numerous and are therefore the main focus of reproduction in this section. In a process called **pollination**, plant anthers release pollen grains and animals and the wind carry the grains to plant carpels.

The sperm is released to fertilize the eggs. Angiosperms reproduce through a method of double fertilization. Two sperm fertilize one ovum. One sperm produces the new plant and the other forms the food supply for the developing plant (endosperm). The ovule develops into a seed and the ovary develops into a fruit. Then the wind or animals carry the seeds to new locations and new plants form in a process called **dispersal**.

The development of the egg to form a plant occurs in three stages: growth, morphogenesis (the development of form), and cellular differentiation (the acquisition of a cell's specific structure and function).

The higher animals use various methods to attract the opposite sex to improve their chances of mating – for example, attractive plumage in birds and various sounds and smells.

Reproduction in animals occurs both asexually and sexually. Reproduction in simple animals like sponges involves simply breaking off a piece of the organism, which in turn develops into an individual. Sexual reproduction occurs by union of egg and sperm.

Fish need water for reproduction. The female fish lay a huge number of eggs and male fish release sperm into the water where fertilization takes place. Most mammals give birth to live offspring and care for them. There are two groups of mammals that are different. The marsupials have a pouch to care for their young and the other group lay eggs from which embryos develop.

0014 Analyze the processes used by living organisms to obtain, store, and use energy

SEE Competency 0010

0015 Analyze the anatomy and physiology of living organisms

Analyze the processes involved in homeostasis

The molecular composition of the immediate environment outside of the organism is not the same as it is inside and the temperature outside may not be optimal for metabolic activity within the organism. **Homeostasis** is the control of these differences between internal and external environments. There are three homeostatic systems to regulate these differences, osmoregulation, excretion, and thermoregulation.

In animals, the kidneys are the site of osmoregulation. **Osmoregulation** is the maintenance of the appropriate level of water and salts in body fluids for optimum cellular functions. The nephrons maintain osmoregulation by repeatedly filtering fluid waste and by reabsorbing excess water. Excretion is the elimination of metabolic (nitrogenous) waste from the body in the form of urea. The functional unit of excretion is the nephron, which make up the kidneys.

Thermoregulation maintains the internal, or core, body temperature of the organism within a tolerable range for metabolic and cellular processes. Common indications of change in body temperature are shivering and sweating. Both are complex behaviors. The site for thermoregulation is the brain. It is the reception site for many hormones and therefore acts as a processing area. It integrates nerve impulses and commands activity.

Compare archaebacteria and eubacteria

Archaebacteria and eubacteria are the two main branches of prokaryotic (moneran) evolution. Archaebacteria evolved from the earliest cells. Most achaebacteria inhabit extreme environments. There are three main groups of archaebacteria: methanogens, extreme halophiles, and extreme thermophiles. Methanogens are strict anaerobes, extreme halophiles live in high salt concentrations, and extreme thermophiles live in hot temperatures (hot springs).

Most prokaryotes fall into the eubacteria (bacteria) domain. Bacteria are divided according to their morphology (shape). Bacilli are rod shaped bacteria, cocci are round bacteria, and spirilli are spiral shaped bacteria.

The Gram stain is a procedure used to differentiate the cell wall make-up of bacteria. Gram positive bacteria have simple cell walls consisting of large amounts of peptidoglycan. These bacteria pick up the stain, revealing a purple color when observed under the microscope. Gram negative bacteria have a more complex cell wall consisting of less peptidoglycan, but have large amounts of lipopolysaccharides. The lipopolysaccharides resist the stain, revealing a pink color when observed under the microscope. Because of the lipopolysaccharide cell wall, Gram negative bacteria tend to be more toxic and are more resistant to antibiotics and host defense mechanisms.

Some bacteria have a sticky capsule that protects the cell wall and is also used for adhesion to surfaces. Pili are surface appendages for adhesion to other cells.

Bacteria locomotion is via flagella or taxis. Taxis is the movement towards or away from a stimulus. The methods for obtaining nutrition are, for photosynthetic organisms or producers, the conversion of sunlight to chemical energy, for consumers or heterotrophs, consumption of other living organisms, and, for saprophytes, consumption of dead or decaying material.

In comparison, archaebacteria contain no peptidoglycan in the cell wall, they are not inhibited by antibiotics, they have several kinds of RNA polymerase, and they do not have a nuclear envelope. Eubacteria (bacteria) have peptidoglycan in the cell wall, they are susceptible to antibiotics, they have one kind of RNA polymerase, and they have no nuclear envelope.

Chromosome and plasmid replication in bacteria

Chromosomal replication in bacteria is similar to eukaryotic DNA replication.

A **plasmid** is a small ring of DNA that carries accessory genes separate from those of a bacterial chromosome. Most plasmids in Gram-negative bacteria undergo bidirectional replication, although some replicate unidirectionally because of their small size. Plasmids in Gram-positive bacteria replicate by the rolling circle mechanism.

Some plasmids can transfer themselves (and therefore their genetic information) by a process called conjugation. Conjugation requires cell-to-cell contact. The sex pilus of the donor cell attaches to the recipient cell. Once contact has been established, the transfer of DNA occurs by the rolling circle mechanism.

Structure and function of protists

Protists are the earliest eukaryotic descendants of prokaryotes. Protists are found almost anywhere there is water. Protists are eukaryotic microorganisms and include the macroscopic algae with only a single tissue type. They are defined by exclusion of characteristics found in other kingdoms. They are not prokaryotes because they have (usually) a true nucleus and membrane-bound organelles. They are not fungi because fungi lack undulopidia and develop from spores. They are not plants because plants develop from embryos and they are not animals because animals develop from a blastula.

Most protists have a true (membrane-bound) nucleus, complex organelles (mitochondria, chloroplasts, etc.), aerobic respiration in mitochondria, and undulipodium (cilia) in some life stage.

The chaotic status of names and concepts of the higher classification of the protists reflects their great diversity of form, function, and life cycles. The protists are often grouped as algae (plant-like), protozoa (animal-like), or fungus-like, based on the similarity of their lifestyle and characteristics to these more clearly defined groups. Two distinctive groups of protists are considered for separation as their own kingdoms. The Archaezoa lack mitochondria, the Golgi apparatus, and have multiple nuclei. The Chromista, including diatoms, brown algae, and "golden" algae with chlorophyll c, have a very different photosynthetic plastid from those found in the green algae and plants.

Knowledge of the significance of fungi, bacteria, and viruses

Although bacteria and fungi may cause disease, they are also beneficial for use as medicines and food. Penicillin is derived from a fungus that is capable of destroying the cell wall of bacteria. In addition, researchers often use viruse and retroviruses as vectors for the delivery of genes to bacteria, plants, and animals in genetic engineering processes (e.g., gene therapy, creation of transgenic organisms).

The majority of prokaryotes decompose material for use by the environment and other organisms. The eukaryotic fungi are the most important decomposers in the biosphere. They break down organic material to be used up by other living organisms.

Compare nonvascular and vascular plants

The **non-vascular plants** represent a grade of evolution characterized by several primitive features for plants: lack of roots, lack of conducting tissues, reliance on absorption of water that falls on the plant or condenses on the plant in high humidity, and a lack of leaves.
Non-vascular plants include the liverworts, hornworts, and mosses. Each is recognized as a separate division.

Defining characteristics of **vascular plants** include:
- Synthesis of lignin to give rigidity and strength to cell walls for growing upright
- Evolution of tracheid cells for water transport and sieve cells for nutrient transport
- The use of underground stems (rhizomes) as a structure from which adventitious roots originate

There are two kinds of vascular plants: non-seeded and seeded. The non-seeded vascular plant divisions include Division Lycophyta (club moses), Division Sphenophyta (horsetails), and Division Pterophyta (ferns). The seeded vascular plants differ from the non-seeded plants by their method of reproduction. The vascular seed plants are divided into two groups, the gymnosperms and the angiosperms.

Gymnosperms were the first plants to evolve using seeds for reproduction, which made them less dependent on water to assist in reproduction. The wind carries their seeds and the pollen from the male. Gymnosperms have cones that protect the seeds.

Gymnosperm divisions include Division Cycadophyta (cycads), Division Ginkgophyta (ginkgo), Division Gnetophyta (gnetophytes), and Division Coniferophyta (conifers).

Angiosperms are the largest group in the plant kingdom. They are the flowering plants and produce true seeds for reproduction. They arose about seventy million years ago when the dinosaurs were disappearing. The land was drying up and the plants' ability to produce seeds that could remain dormant until conditions became acceptable allowed for their success. They also have more advanced vascular tissue and larger leaves for increased photosynthesis. Angiosperms consist of only one division, the Anthrophyta. Angiosperms are divided into monocots and dicots. Monocots have one cotelydon (seed leaf) and parallel veins on their leaves. Their flower petals are in multiples of threes. Dicots have two cotelydons and branching veins on their leaves. Flower petals are in multiples of fours or fives.

Plant anatomy and physiology

Roots, stems, leaves, and reproductive structures are the most functionally important parts of plant anatomy. Different types of plants have distinctive anatomical structures.

Roots absorb water and minerals and exchange gases in the soil. Like stems, roots contain xylem and phloem. The xylem transports water and minerals, called xylem sap, upwards. The sugar produced by photosynthesis goes down the phloem in the phloem sap, traveling to the roots and other non-photosynthetic parts of the plant. In addition to water and mineral absorption, roots anchor plants in place preventing erosion.

Stems are the major support structure of plants. Stems consist primarily of three types of tissue: dermal tissue, ground tissue, and vascular tissue. Dermal tissue covers the outside surface of the stem to prevent excessive water loss and control gas exchange. Ground tissue consists mainly of parenchyma cells and surrounds the vascular tissue providing support and protection. Finally, vascular tissue, xylem and phloem, provides long distance transport of nutrients and water.

Leaves enable plants to capture light and carbon dioxide for photosynthesis. Photosynthesis occurs primarily in the leaves. Plants exchange gases through their leaves via stomata, small openings on the underside of the leaves. Stomata allow oxygen to move in or out of the plant and carbon dioxide to move in. Leaf size and shape varies greatly between species of plants and botanists often identify plants by their characteristic leaf patterns.

Reproductive Structures

The sporophyte is the dominant phase in reproduction. Sporophytes contain a diploid set of chromosomes and form haploid spores by meiosis. Spores develop into gametophytes that produce gametes by mitosis. Angiosperm reproductive structures are the flowers.

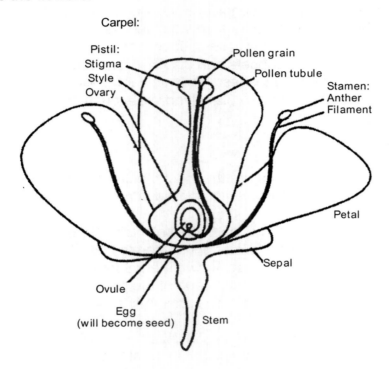

The male gametophytes are pollen grains and the female gametophytes are embryo sacs that are inside of the ovules. The male pollen grains form in the anthers at the tips of the stamens. The ovaries contain the female ovules. Finally, the stamen is the reproductive organ of the male and the carpel is the reproductive organ of the female.

Recognize evolutionary and adaptive significance of plant structures

Plants require adaptations that allow them to absorb light for photosynthesis. Since they are unable to move about, they must evolve methods to allow them to reproduce successfully. As time passed, the plants moved from a water environment to the land. Advantages of life on land included more available light and a higher concentration of carbon dioxide. Originally, there were no predators and less competition for space on land. Plants had to evolve methods of support, reproduction, respiration, and conservation of water once they moved to land. A division of labor among plant tissues evolved in order to obtain water and minerals from the earth. A wax cuticle is produced to prevent the loss of water. Leaves enabled plants to capture light and carbon dioxide for photosynthesis. Stomata provide openings on the underside of leaves for oxygen to move in or out of the plant and for carbon dioxide to move in. A method of anchorage (roots) evolved. Finally, the polymer lignin evolved to give tremendous strength to plants.

Identify the general characteristics of vertebrate and invertebrate development

Animal tissue becomes specialized during development. The ectoderm (outer layer) becomes the epidermis or skin. The mesoderm (middle layer) becomes muscles and other organs beside the gut. The endoderm (inner layer) becomes the gut, also called the archenteron.

Sponges are the simplest animals and lack true tissue. They exhibit no symmetry.

Diploblastic animals have only two germ layers: the ectoderm and endoderm. They have no true digestive system. Diploblastic animals include the Cnideria (jellyfish). They exhibit radial symmetry.

Triploblastic animals have all three germ layers. Triploblastic animals can be further divided into: Acoelomates, Pseudocoelomates, and Coelomates.

> **Acoelomates** have no defined body cavity. An example is the flatworm (Platyhelminthe), which must absorb food from a host's digestive system.

> **Pseudocoelomates** have a body cavity that is not lined by tissue from the mesoderm. An example is the roundworm (Nematoda).

Coelomates have a true fluid filled body cavity called a coelom derived from the mesoderm. Coelomates can further be divided into protostomes and deuterostomes. In the development of protostomes, the first opening becomes the mouth and the second opening becomes the anus. The mesoderm splits to form the coelom. In the development of deuterostomes, the mouth develops from the second opening and the anus from the first opening. The mesoderm hollows out to become the coelom. Protostomes include animals in the phyla Mollusca, Annelida, and Arthropoda. Deuterostomes include animals in phyla Ehinodermata and Vertebrata.

Development is a change in form. Animals go through several stages of development after fertilization of the egg cell: cleavage, blastula, gastrulation, neuralation, and organogenesis.

Cleavage - the first divisions of the fertilized egg. Cleavage continues until the egg becomes a blastula.
Blastula - a hollow ball of undifferentiated cells.
Gastrulation - the time of tissue differentiation into the separate germ layers, the endoderm, mesoderm, and ectoderm.
Neuralation - development of the nervous system.
Organogenesis - the development of the various organs of the body.

Knowledge of physiological processes of animals

Animals constantly require oxygen for cellular respiration and need to remove carbon dioxide from their bodies. The respiratory surface must be large and moist. Different animal groups have different types of respiratory organs to perform gas exchange. Some animals (e.g. worms) use their entire outer skin for respiration. Fish and other aquatic animals have gills for gas exchange. Ventilation increases the flow of water over the gills. This process supplies oxygen and removes carbon dioxide. Fish use a large amount of energy to ventilate their gills. This is because the oxygen available in water is less than that available in the air. The arthropoda (insects) have tracheal tubes that send air to all parts of their bodies.

Diffusion is the mechanism of gas exchange for smaller insects. Larger insects ventilate their bodies by a series of body movements that compress and expand the tracheal tubes. Vertebrates have lungs as their primary respiratory organ. The gas exchange system in all vertebrates is similar to that in humans.

Osmoregulation and excretion in many invertebrates involves tubular systems. The tubules branch throughout the body. Interstitial fluid enters these tubes and is collected into excretory ducts that empty into the external environment through openings in the body wall. Insects have excretory organs called Malpighian tubes. These organs pump water, salts, and nitrogenous waste into the tubules.
These fluids then pass through the hindgut and out the rectum. In vertebrates, kidneys are the primary excretion organs.

Analyze the importance of animal behaviors

Animal behavior includes courtship leading to mating, communication between species, territoriality, aggression between animals, and dominance within a group. Animal communication is any behavior by one animal that affects the behavior of another animal. Animals use body language, sound, and smell to communicate. Perhaps the most common type of animal communication is the presentation or movement of distinctive body parts. Many species of animals reveal or conceal body parts to communicate with potential mates, predators, and prey. In addition, many species of animals communicate with sound. Examples of vocal communication include the mating "songs" of birds and frogs and warning cries of monkeys. Finally, many animals release scented chemicals called pheromones and secrete distinctive odors from specialized glands to communicate with other animals.

Pheromones are important in reproduction and mating and glandular secretions of long lasting smells alert animals to the presence of others.

Innate behaviors are inborn or instinctual. An environmental stimulus such as the length of day or temperature results in a behavior. Hibernation among some animals is an innate behavior. **Learned behavior** is modified due to past experience.

Subarea IV. Human Biology

0016 Understand the structures and functions of the human skeleton, muscular, and integumentary systems

The Human Skeleton

The axial skeleton consists of the bones of the skull and vertebrae. The appendicular skeleton consists of the bones of the legs, arms, tail, and shoulder girdle. Bone is a connective tissue.

Parts of the bone include compact bone that gives strength, spongy bone that contains red marrow to make blood cells and yellow marrow in the center of long bones to store fat cells, and the periosteum that is the protective covering on the outside of the bone.

In addition to bones and muscles, ligaments and tendons are important joint components. A joint is a place where two bones meet. Joints enable movement. Ligaments attach bone to bone. Tendons attach bone to muscle. There are three types of joints:

1.   Ball and socket – allow for rotational movement. An example is the joint between the shoulder and the upper arm bone (humerus). These joints allow humans to move their arms and legs in many different ways.
2.   Hinge – restricts movement to a single plane. An example is the joint between the humerus and the forearm (ulna).
3.   Pivot – allows for the rotation of the forearm at the elbow and the hands at the wrist.

The Muscular System

The function of the muscular system is to facilitate movement. There are three types of muscle tissue: skleletal, cardiac, and smooth.

Skeletal muscle is voluntary. These muscles attachto bones and are responsible for their movement. Skeletal muscle consists of long fibers and is striated due to the repeating patterns of the myofilaments (made of the proteins actin and myosin) that make up the fibers. The mechanism of skeletal muscle contraction involves a nerve impulse striking a muscle fiber. This causes calcium ions to flood the sarcomere. The myosin fibers creep along the actin, causing the muscle to contract. Once the nerve impulse has passed, calcium is pumped out and the contraction ends.

Cardiac muscle is found in the heart. Cardiac muscle is striated like skeletal muscle, but differs in that the plasma membrane of the cardiac muscle causes the muscle to beat even when away from the heart. The action potentials of cardiac and skeletal muscles also differ.

Smooth muscle is involuntary. It is found in organs and enable functions such as digestion and respiration. Unlike skeletal and cardiac muscle, smooth muscle is not striated. Smooth muscle has less myosin and does not generate as much tension as the striated muscles.

The Integumentary System

The integumentary system is the body's external covering that includes the skin, hair, nails, sweat glands, and mucous.

The skin consists of two distinct layers. The epidermis is the thinner outer layer and the dermis is the thicker inner layer. Layers of tightly packed epithelial cells make up the epidermis. The tight packaging of the epithelial cells supports the skin's function as a protective barrier against infection.

The top layer of the epidermis consists of dead skin cells and is filled with keratin, a waterproofing protein. The dermis layer consists of connective tissue. It contains blood vessels, hair follicles, sweat glands, and sebaceous glands. An oily secretion called sebum, produced by the sebaceous gland, is released to the outer epidermis through the hair follicles. Sebum maintains the pH of the skin between 3 and 5, which inhibits most microorganism growth.

The skin also plays a role in thermoregulation. Increased body temperature causes skin blood vessels to dilate, resulting in heat radiating from the skin's surface. The sweat glands also activate, increasing evaporative cooling. Decreased body temperature causes skin blood vessels to constrict. This results in blood from the skin diverting to deeper tissues and reduces heat loss from the surface of the skin.

0017 Understand the structures and functions of the human circulatory and immune systems

Analyze the structure, function, and regulation of the heart

The function of the closed circulatory system (**cardiovascular system**) is to carry oxygenated blood and nutrients to all cells of the body and return carbon dioxide waste to be expelled from the lungs. The heart, blood vessels, and blood make up the cardiovascular system. The figure below shows the structure of the heart:

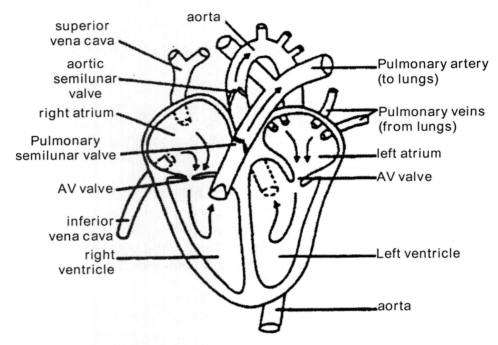

The atria are the chambers that receive blood returning to the heart and the ventricles are the chambers that pump blood out of the heart. There are four valves, two atrioventricular (AV) valves and two semilunar valves. The AV valves are located between each atrium and ventricle. The contraction of the ventricles closes the AV valve to keep blood from flowing back into the atria. The semilunar valves are located where the aorta leaves the left ventricle and the pulmonary artery leaves the right ventricle. The semilunar valves are opened by ventricular contraction to allow blood to be pumped out into the arteries and closed by the relaxation of the ventricles.

The cardiac output is the volume of blood per minute that the left ventricle pumps. This output depends on the heart rate and stroke volume. The **heart rate** is the number of times the heart beats per minute and the **stroke volume** is the amount of blood pumped by the left ventricle each time it contracts. Humans have an average cardiac output of about 5.25 L/min. Heavy exercise can increase cardiac output up to five times. Epinephrine and increased body temperature also increase heart rate and cardiac output.

Cardiac muscle can contract without any signal from the nervous system. It is the sinoatrial node that is the pacemaker of the heart. It is located on the wall of the right atrium and generates electrical impulses that make the cardiac muscle cells contract in unison. The atrioventricular node briefly delays the electrical impulse to ensure the atria empty before the ventricles contract.

Understand the influence of changes on the circulatory system

There are three kinds of blood vessels in the circulatory system: arteries, capillaries, and veins. **Arteries** carry oxygenated blood away from the heart to organs in the body. Arteries branch off to form smaller arterioles in the organs. The arterioles form tiny **capillaries** that reach every tissue. At their downstream end, capillaries combine to form larger venules. Venules combine to form larger **veins** that return blood to the heart. Arteries and veins differ in the direction in which they carry blood.

Blood vessels are lined by endothelial cells. In veins and arteries, a layer of smooth muscle and an outer layer of elastic connective tissue surrounds the endothelium. Capillaries consist only of the thin endothelium layer and its basement membrane that allows for nutrient absorption.

Blood flow velocity decreases as it reaches the capillaries. The capillaries have the smallest diameter of all the blood vessels, but this is not why the velocity decreases. Arteries carry blood to such a large number of capillaries, the blood flow velocity actually decelerates as it enters the capillaries. Blood pressure is the hydrostatic force that blood exerts against the wall of a vessel. Blood pressure is greater in arteries. It is the force that conveys blood from the heart through the arteries and capillaries.

Blood is a connective tissue consisting of the liquid plasma and several kinds of cells. Approximately 60% of the blood is plasma. It contains water salts called electrolytes, nutrients, waste, and proteins. The electrolytes maintain a pH of about 7.4. The proteins contribute to blood viscosity and helps maintain pH. Some of the proteins are immunoglobulins, the antibodies that help fend off infection. Another group of proteins are clotting factors.

The lymphatic system is responsible for returning lost fluid and proteins to the blood. Fluid enters lymph capillaries. This lymph fluid is filtered in the lymph nodes that contain white blood cells that fight off infection.

The two classes of cells in blood are red blood cells and white blood cells. **Red blood cells (erythrocytes)** are the most numerous. They contain hemoglobin, which carries oxygen. **White blood cells (leukocytes)** are larger than red blood cells. They are phagocytic and can engulf invaders. White blood cells are not confined to the blood vessels and can enter the interstitial fluid between cells.

There are five types of white blood cells: monocytes, neutophils, basophils, eosinophils, and lymphocytes.

A third cellular element found in blood is platelets. **Platelets** are made in the bone marrow and assist in blood clotting. The neurotransmitter that initiates blood vessel constriction following an injury is called serotonin. A material called prothrombin is converted to thrombin with the help of thromboplastin. Thrombin is then used to convert fibrinogen to fibrin, which traps red blood cells to form a scab and stop blood flow.

Malfunctions of the circulatory system

Cardiovascular diseases are the leading cause of death in the United States. Cardiac disease usually results in either a heart attack or stroke. A heart attack is when cardiac muscle tissue dies, usually from coronary artery blockage. A stroke is when nervous tissue in the brain dies due to the blockage of arteries in the head.

A disease called atherosclerosis causes many heart attacks and strokes. Plaques form on the inner walls of arteries, narrowing the area in which blood can flow. Arteriosclerosis is when the arteries harden from plaque accumulation. A healthy diet that limits lipids and cholesterol and regular exercise can prevent atherosclerosis. High blood pressure (hypertension) promotes atherosclerosis. Diet, medication, and exercise can reduce high blood pressure and prevent atherosclerosis.

Structure, function, and regulation of the immune system

The immune system is responsible for defending the body against foreign invaders. There are two defense mechanisms: non specific and specific.

The **non-specific** immune mechanism has two lines of defenses. The first line of defense is the physical barriers of the body. These include the skin and mucous membranes. The skin prevents the penetration of bacteria and viruses. Mucous membranes form a protective barrier around the digestive, respiratory, and genitourinary tracts. In addition, the pH of the skin and mucous membranes inhibit the growth of many microbes. Mucous secretions (tears and saliva) wash away many microbes and contain lysozyme that kills many organisms.
The second line of defense includes white blood cells and the inflammatory response. **Phagocytosis** is the ingestion of foreign particles. Neutrophils make up about seventy percent of all white blood cells. Monocytes mature to become macrophages which are the largest phagocytic cells.

Eosinophils are also phagocytic. Natural killer cells destroy the body's own infected cells instead of the invading microbe directly.

The other second line of defense is the inflammatory response. After injury, the blood supply increases to the injured area, causing redness and heat. Swelling also typically occurs with inflammation. Basophils and mast cells release histamine when the cells are injured. This triggers the inflammatory response.

The **specific** immune mechanism recognizes specific foreign material and responds by destroying the invader. These mechanisms are specific and diverse. They are able to recognize individual pathogens. An **antigen** is any foreign particle that elicits an immune response. An **antibody** is manufactured by the body and recognizes and latches onto antigens, hopefully destroying them. They also differentiate between foreign material and the self. Memory of the invaders provides immunity upon further exposure.

Immunity is the body's ability to recognize and destroy an antigen before it causes harm. Active immunity develops after recovery from an infectious disease (e.g. chicken pox) or after a vaccination (e.g., mumps, measles, rubella). Passive immunity may be passed from one individual to another and is not permanent. A good example is the immunities that a mother passes to her nursing child. A baby's immune system is not well developed and the passive immunity they receive through nursing keeps them healthier.

There are two main responses made by the body after exposure to an antigen: humoral and cell-mediated.

1. **Humoral response** - Free antigens activate this response. B cells (lymphocytes from bone marrow) give rise to plasma cells that secrete antibodies and memory cells that will recognize future exposures to the same antigen. The antibodies defend against extracellular pathogens by binding to the antigen and making them an easy target for phagocytes to engulf and destroy. Antibodies are in a class of proteins called immunoglobulins. There are five major classes of immunoglobulins (Ig) involved in the humoral response: IgM, IgG, IgA, IgD, and IgE.

2. **Cell-mediated response** – Infected cells that have been infected activate T cells (lymphocytes from the thymus). These activated T cells defend against pathogens in the cells or cancer cells by binding to the infected cells and destroying them along with the antigen. T cell receptors on the T helper cells recognize antigens bound to the body's own cells. T helper cells release IL-2, which stimulates other lymphocytes (cytotoxic T cells and B cells). Cytotoxic T cells kill infected host cells by recognizing specific antigens.

Vaccines are antigens given in very small amounts. They stimulate both humoral and cell-mediated responses and help memory cells recognize future exposure to the antigen for more rapid production of antibodies.

Malfunctions of the immune system

The immune system attacks not only microbes, but also cells that are not native to the host. This is the problem with skin grafts, organ transplantations, and blood transfusions. Antibodies to foreign blood and tissue types already exist in the body. If transfused blood is not compatible with the host, these antibodies destroy the new blood cells. There is a similar reaction associated with tissue and organ transplants.

The major histocompatibility complex (MHC) is responsible for the rejection of tissue and organ transplants. This complex is unique to each person. Cytotoxic T cells recognize the MHC on the transplanted tissue or organ as foreign and destroy these tissues. Various drugs are needed to suppress the immune system so this does not happen. The problem is that the patient is now more susceptible to infection.

Autoimmune disease occurs when the body's own immune system destroys its own cells. Lupus, Grave's disease, and rheumatoid arthritis are examples of autoimmune diseases. There is no way to prevent autoimmune diseases. Immunodeficiency is a deficiency in either the humoral or cell-mediated immune defenses. HIV is an example of an immunodeficiency disease.

0018 Understand the structures and functions of the human respiratory and excretory systems

Surface area, volume, and function of the respiratory and excretory systems

The lungs are the respiratory surface of the human respiratory system. A dense net of capillaries contained just beneath the epithelium forms the respiratory surface. The surface area of the epithelium is about 100 m^2 in humans. Based on the surface area, the volume of air inhaled and exhaled is the tidal volume. This is normally about 500mL in adults. Vital capacity is the maximum volume the lungs can inhale and exhale. This is usually around 3400mL.

The kidneys are the primary organs in the excretory system. The pair of kidneys in humans are each about 10cm long. They receive about 20% of the blood pumped with each heartbeat despite their small size. The function of the excretory system is to rid the body of nitrogenous wastes in the form of urea.

Knowledge of process of breathing and gas exchange

The respiratory system functions in the gas exchange of oxygen and carbon dioxide waste. It delivers oxygen to the bloodstream and picks up carbon dioxide for release from the body. Air enters the mouth and nose, where it is warmed, moistened, and filtered of dust and particles. Cilia in the trachea trap unwanted material in mucus, which can be expelled. The trachea splits into two bronchial tubes and the bronchial tubes divide into smaller and smaller bronchioles in the lungs. The internal surface of the lung is composed of alveoli, which are thin walled air sacs. These allow for a large surface area for gas exchange. The alveoli are lined with capillaries. Oxygen diffuses into the bloodstream and carbon dioxide diffuses out of the capillaries to be exhaled out of the lungs.

The oxygenated blood is carried to the heart and delivered to all parts of the body by hemoglobin, a protein consisting of iron.

The thoracic cavity holds the lungs. The diaphragm muscle below the lungs is an adaptation that makes inhalation possible. As the volume of the thoracic cavity increases, the diaphragm muscle flattens out and inhalation occurs.

Knowledge of osmoregulation and waste removal

The functional unit of excretion is the nephron, which makes up the kidneys. The structures of the excretory system and the nephron are as follows:

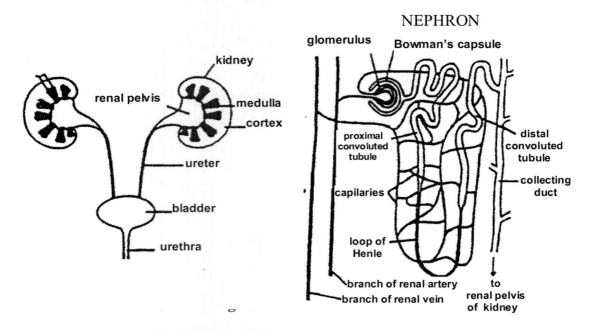

The Bowman's capsule contains the glomerulus, a tightly packed group of capillaries in the nephron. The glomerulus is under high pressure. Water, urea, salts, and other fluids leak out due to pressure into the Bowman's capsule. This fluid waste (filtrate) passes through the three regions of the nephron: the proximal convulated tubule, the loop of Henle, and the distal tubule. In the proximal convoluted tubule, unwanted molecules are secreted into the filtrate. In the loop of Henle, salt is actively pumped out of the tube and water is lost due to the hyperosmosity of the inner part (medulla) of the kidney. As the fluid enters the distal tubule, more water is reabsorbed. Urine forms in the collecting duct that leads to the ureter then to the bladder where it is stored. Urine is passed from the bladder through the urethra. The amount of water reabsorbed back into the body is dependent upon how much water or fluids an individual has consumed. Urine can be very dilute or very concentrated depending on the level of concentration.

Malfunctions of the respiratory and excretory systems

Emphysema is a chronic obstructive pulmonary disease (COPD). Such diseases make breathing difficult because airflow through the bronchial tubes is partially blocked. The primary cause of emphysema is cigarette smoke. People with a deficiency in alpha$_1$-antitrypsin protein production have a greater risk of developing emphysema and at an earlier age. This protein helps protect the lungs from damage done by inflammation. This genetic deficiency is rare and can be tested for in individuals with a family history of the deficiency. There is no cure for emphysema, but there are treatments available. The best prevention against emphysema is to avoid smoking.

Nephritis usually occurs in children. Symptoms include hypertension, decreased renal function, hematuria, and edema. Glomerulonephritis (GN) generally is a more precise term to describe this disease. Nephritis is produced by an antigen-antibody complex that causes inflammation and cell proliferation. Normal kidney tissue is damaged and, if left untreated, nephritis can lead to kidney failure and death.

0019 Understand the principles of human nutrition and structures and functions of the human digestive system

Understand the roles of basic nutrients found in foods

The function of the digestive system is to break down food into nutrients and absorb them into the blood stream where they can be delivered to all cells of the body for use in cellular respiration.

Essential nutrients are those nutrients that the body needs but cannot make. There are four groups of essential nutrients: essential amino acids, essential fatty acids, vitamins, and minerals.

There are ten essential amino acids humans need. A lack of these amino acids results in protein deficiency. There are only a few essential fatty acids.

Vitamins are organic molecules essential for a nutritionally adequate diet. Nutritionists have identified thirteen vitamins essential to humans.

There are two groups of vitamins: water soluble (includes the vitamin B complex and vitamin C) and water insoluble (vitamins A, D and K). Vitamin deficiencies can cause severe health problems.

Unlike vitamins, minerals are inorganic molecules. Calcium is needed for bone construction and maintenance. Iron is important in cellular respiration and is a major component of hemoglobin.

Carbohydrates, fats, and proteins are fuel for the generation of ATP. Water is necessary to keep the body hydrated.

Understand mechanical and chemical digestion

The teeth and saliva begin digestion by breaking food down into smaller pieces and lubricating them so they can be swallowed. The lips, cheeks, and tongue form a bolus or ball of food. It is carried down the pharynx by the process of peristalsis (wave-like contractions) and enters the stomach through the sphincter, which closes to keep food from going back up. In the stomach, pepsinogen and hydrochloric acid form pepsin, the enzyme that hydrolyzes proteins. The food is broken down further by this chemical action and is churned into acid chyme. The pyloric sphincter muscle opens to allow the food to enter the small intestine.

Most nutrient absorption occurs in the small intestine. Its large surface area, resulting from its length and protrusions called villi and microvilli, allow for a great absorptive surface into the bloodstream. Chyme is neutralized after coming from the acidic stomach to allow the enzymes found there to function. Accessory organs function in the production of necessary enzymes and bile. The pancreas makes many enzymes to break down food in the small intestine. The liver makes bile, which breaks down and emulsifies fatty acids. Any food left after the trip through the small intestine enters the large intestine. The large intestine functions to reabsorb water and produce vitamin K. The feces, or remaining waste, are passed out through the anus.

Malfunctions of the digestive system

Gastric ulcers are lesions in the stomach lining. Bacteria are the main cause of ulcers, but pepsin and acid worsen the condition if the ulcers do not heal quickly enough.

Appendicitis is the inflammation of the appendix. The appendix has no known function, is open to the intestine, and can be blocked by hardened stool or swollen tissue. The blocked appendix can cause bacterial infections and inflammation leading to appendicitis. The swelling cuts the blood supply, killing the organ tissue. If left untreated, this leads to the rupture of the appendix, allowing the stool and infection to spill out into the abdomen. This condition is life threatening without immediate surgery. Symptoms of appendicitis include lower abdominal pain, nausea, loss of appetite, and fever.

0020   Understand the structures and functions of the human nervous system and endocrine systems

Knowledge of the central and peripheral nervous systems

The **central nervous system** (CNS) consists of the brain and spinal cord. The CNS is responsible for the body's response to environmental stimuli. The spinal cord is located inside the spine. It sends out motor commands for movement in response to stimuli. The brain is where responses to more complex stimuli occurs. The meninges are the connective tissues that protect the CNS. The CNS contains fluid filled spaces called ventricles. The fluid cushions the brain and circulates nutrients, white blood cells, and hormones. Tv v b he CNS's response to stimuli is a reflex. The reflex is an unconscious, automatic response.

The **peripheral nervous system (PNS)** consists of the nerves that connect the CNS to the rest of the body. The sensory division brings information to the CNS from sensory receptors and the motor division sends signals from the CNS to effector cells. The motor division consists of somatic nervous system and the autonomic nervous system. The somatic nervous system is controlled consciously in response to external stimuli. The autonomic nervous system is unconsciously controlled by the hypothalamus of the brain to regulate the internal environment. This system is responsible for the movement of smooth and cardiac muscles as well as the muscles for other organ systems.

Analyze the role of nerve impulses and neurons

The **neuron** is the basic unit of the nervous system. It consists of an axon, which carries impulses away from the cell body to the tip of the neuron; the dendrite, which carries impulses toward the cell body; and the cell body, which contains the nucleus. Synapses are spaces between neurons. Chemicals called neurotransmitters are found close to the synapse. The myelin sheath, composed of Schwann cells, covers the neurons and provides insulation.

Nerve action depends on depolarization and an imbalance of electrical charges across the neuron. A polarized nerve has a positive charge outside the neuron. A depolarized nerve has a negative charge outside the neuron.

Neurotransmitters turn off the sodium pump, which results in depolarization of the membrane. This wave of depolarization (as it moves from neuron to neuron) carries an electrical impulse. This is actually a wave of opening and closing gates that allows the flow of ions across the synapse. Nerves have an action potential. There is a threshold of the level of chemicals that must be met or exceeded in order for muscles to respond. This is called an "all or none" response.

Understand the major endocrine glands and the function of their hormones

The function of the **endocrine system** is to manufacture proteins called hormones. **Hormones** are released into the bloodstream and are carried to a target tissue where they stimulate an action. There are two classes of hormones: steroid and peptide. Steroid hormones come from cholesterol and include the sex hormones. Peptide hormones are derived from amino acids. Hormones are specific and fit receptors on the target tissue cell surface. The receptor activates an enzyme that converts ATP to cyclic AMP. Cyclic AMP (cAMP) is a second messenger from the cell membrane to the nucleus. The genes found in the nucleus turn on or off to cause a specific response.

Endocrine cells, which make up endocrine glands, secrete hormones. The major endocrine glands and their hormones are:

> **Hypothalamus** – located in the lower brain, signals the pituitary gland.
> **Pituitary gland** – located at the base of the hypothalamus, releases growth hormones and antidiuretic hormones (causing retention of water in kidneys).
> **Thyroid gland** – located on the trachea, lowers blood calcium levels (calcitonin) and maintains metabolic processes (thyroxine).
> **Gonads** – located in the testes of the male and the ovaries of the female, testes release androgens to support sperm formation and ovaries release estrogens and progesterone to stimulate and promote uterine lining growth.
> **Pancreas** – secretes insulin to lower blood glucose levels and glucagon to raise blood glucose levels.

Understand the feedback mechanisms in homeostasis

The thyroid gland produces hormones that help maintain heart rate, blood pressure, muscle tone, digestion, and reproductive functions. The parathyroid glands maintain the calcium level in blood and the pancreas maintains glucose homeostasis by secreting insulin and glucagon. The three gonadal steroids, androgen (testosterone), estrogen, and progesterone, regulate the development of the male and female reproductive organs.

Neurotransmitters are chemical messengers. The most common neurotransmitter is acetylcholine. Acetylcholine controls muscle contraction and heartbeat. A group of neurotransmitters, the catecholamines, include epinephrine and norepinephrine. Epinephrine (adrenaline) and norepinephrine are also hormones. They are produced in response to stress. They have profound effects on the cardiovascular and respiratory systems. These hormones/neurotransmitters can be used to increase the rate and stroke volume of the heart, thus increasing the rate of oxygen delivery to the blood cells.

Malfunctions of the nervous and endocrine systems

Diabetes is the best known endocrine disorder. A deficiency of insulin resulting in high blood glucose causes diabetes. Type I diabetes is an autoimmune disorder. The immune system attacks the cells of the pancreas, inhibiting insulin production. Treatment for type I diabetes consists of daily insulin injections. Type II diabetes usually occurs with age and/or obesity. There is usually a reduced response in target cells due to changes in insulin receptors or a deficiency of insulin. Type II diabetics need to monitor their blood glucose levels. Treatment usually includes dietary restrictions and exercise.

Hyperthyroidism is another disorder of the endocrine system, resulting in excessive secretion of thyroid hormones. Symptoms are weight loss, high blood pressure, and high body temperature. The opposite condition, hypothyroidism, causes weight gain, lethargy, and intolerance to cold.

There are many nervous system disorders including Alzheimer's disease, Amyotrophic Lateral Sclerosis (ALS or Lou Gehrig's disease), Huntington's disease, and Parkinson's disease. Parkinson's disease is caused by the degeneration of the basal ganglia in the brain. This causes a breakdown in the transmission of motor impulses to the muscles. Like many neurodegenerative diseases, there is no cure for Parkinson's.

0021 Understand the structures and functions of the human reproductive systems and the processes of embryonic development

Understand hormone control and development and function of male and female reproductive systems

Hormones regulate sexual maturation in humans. Humans cannot reproduce until about the puberty age of 8-14, depending on the individual. The hypothalamus begins secreting hormones that stimulate maturation of the reproductive system and development of the secondary sex characteristics. Reproductive maturity in girls occurs with their first menstruation and occurs in boys with the first ejaculation of viable sperm.

Hormones also regulate reproduction. In males, the primary sex hormones are the androgens, testosterone being the most important. The androgens are produced in the testes and are responsible for the primary and secondary sex characteristics of the male. Female hormone patterns are cyclic and complex. Most women have a reproductive cycle length of about 28 days. The menstrual cycle is specific to the changes in the uterus. The ovarian cycle results in ovulation and occurs in parallel with the menstrual cycle. Hormones regulate this parallelism. Five hormones participate in this regulation, most notably estrogen and progesterone. Estrogen and progesterone play an important role in the signaling to the uterus and the development and maintenance of the endometruim. Estrogens are also responsible for the secondary sex characteristics of females.

Gametogenesis, fertilization, and birth control

Gametogenesis is the production of the sperm and egg cells.

Spermatogenesis begins at puberty in the male. One spermatogonia, the diploid precursor of sperm, produces four sperm. The sperm mature in the seminiferous tubules located in the testes. **Oogenesis**, the production of egg cells (ova), is usually complete by the birth of a female. Egg cells are not released until menstruation begins at puberty. Meiosis forms one ovum with all the cytoplasm and three polar bodies that the body reabsorbs. The ova are stored in the ovaries and released each month from puberty to menopause.

Sperm are stored in the seminiferous tubules in the testes where they mature. Mature sperm are found in the epididymis located on top of the testes. After ejaculation, the sperm travel up the **vas deferens** where they mix with semen made in the prostate and seminal vesicles and travel out the urethra.

Ovulation releases the egg into the fallopian tubes that contain cilia to help move the egg along. Fertilization of the egg by the sperm normally occurs in the fallopian tubes. If pregnancy does not occur, the egg passes through the uterus and is expelled through the vagina during menstruation. Levels of progesterone and estrogen stimulate menstruation and are negatively affected by the implantation of a fertilized egg, thus preventing menstruation after egg implantation.

There are many methods of contraception (birth control) that affect different stages of fertilization. Oral contraceptives (birth control pills) prevent ovulation by introducting synthetic estrogen and progesterone. Several barrier methods of contraception are available. Male and female condoms block semen from contacting the egg. Sterilization is another method of birth control. Tubil ligation in women prevents eggs from entering the uterus. A vasectomy in men involves the cutting of the vas deferens. This prevents the sperm from entering the urethra.

Embryonic and fetal development

If fertilization occurs, the zygote begins dividing about 24 hours later. The resulting cells form a blastocyst that implants within two to three days in the uterus. Implantation promotes secretion of human chorionic gonadotrophin (HCG). This is what is detected in pregnancy tests. The HCG keeps the level of progesterone elevated to maintain the uterine lining in order to feed the developing embryo until the umbilical cord forms.

Organogenesis, the development of the body organs, occurs during the first trimester of fetal development. The heart begins to beat and all the major structures are present at this time. The fetus grows very rapidly during the second trimester of pregnancy. The fetus is about 30 cm long and is very active at this stage. During the third and last trimester, fetal activity may decrease as the fetus grows. Labor is initiated by oxytocin, which causes labor contractions and dilation of the cervix. Prolactin and oxytocin cause the production of milk.

Subarea V.   Principles of Heredity and the Evolution of Life

0022   Understand the principles of Mendelian and non-Mendelian genetics

Understand the basic principles of heredity

Gregor Mendel is recognized as the father of genetics. His work in the late 1800's is the basis of our knowledge of genetics. Although unaware of the presence of DNA or genes, Mendel realized there were factors (now known as **genes**) parents transfer to their offspring. Mendel worked with pea plants and fertilized the plants himself, keeping track of subsequent generations which led to the Mendelian laws of genetics. Mendel found that two "factors" governed each trait, one from each parent. Traits or characteristics came in several forms, known as **alleles**. For example, the trait of flower color had white alleles (*pp*) and purple alleles (*PP*).   Mendel formulated two laws: the law of segregation and the law of independent assortment.

The **law of segregation** states that only one of the two possible alleles from each parent is passed on to the offspring. If the two alleles differ, then one is fully expressed in the organism's appearance (the dominant allele) and the other has no noticeable effect on appearance (the recessive allele). The two alleles for each trait segregate into different gametes. A Punnet square can be used to show the law of segregation. In a Punnet square, one parent's genes are put at the top of the box and the other parent's on the side. Genes combine in the squares just like numbers are added in addition tables. This Punnet square shows the result of the cross of two first generation (F_1) hybrids.

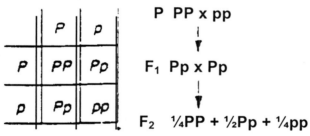

P PP x pp

F_1 Pp x Pp

F_2 ¼PP + ½Pp + ¼pp

This cross results in a 1:2:1 ratio of second generation (F_2) offspring. Here, the *P* is the dominant allele and the *p* is the recessive allele. The F_1 cross produces three offspring expressing the dominant allele (two *PP* and *Pp*) and one offspring expressing the recessive allele (*pp*). Some other important terms to know:

Homozygous – having a pair of identical alleles. For example, *PP* and *pp* flowers are homozygous.
Heterozygous – having two different alleles. For example, *Pp* flowers are heterozygous.
Phenotype – the organism's physical appearance.
Genotype – the organism's genetic make-up. For example, *PP* and *Pp* flowers have the same phenotype (purple in color), but different genotypes.

BIOLOGY   71

The **law of independent assortment** states that alleles assort independently of each other. The law of segregation applies for monohybrid crosses (only one character, in this case flower color, is experimented with). Dihybrid crosses explore two characters. Two of the seven characters Mendel studied were seed shape and color. Yellow is the dominant seed color (*Y*) and green is the recessive color (*y*). The dominant seed shape is round (*R*) and the recessive shape is wrinkled (*r*). A cross between a plant with yellow round seeds (*YYRR*) and a plant with green wrinkled seeds (*yyrr*) produces an F_1 generation with the genotype *YyRr*. The production of F_2 offspring results in a 9:3:3:1 phenotypic ratio.

F_2

	YR	Yr	yR	yr
YR	YYRR	YYRr	YyRR	YyRr
Yr	YYRr	YYrr	YyRr	Yyrr
yR	YyRR	YyRr	yyRR	yyRr
yr	YyRr	Yyrr	yyRr	yyrr

P   YYRR x yyrr
↓
F_1 YyRr
↓

F_2 YYRR – 1 ⎫
         YYRr – 2 ⎬ 9 yellow round
         YyRR – 2 ⎪
         YyRr – 4 ⎭

         yyRR – 1 ⎫ 3 green round
         yyRr – 2 ⎭

         YYrr – 1 ⎫ 3 yellow wrinkled
         Yyrr – 2 ⎭

         yyrr – 1 } 1 green wrinkled

Mendelian genetics allowed the discovery of the more complex hereditary pattern of **dominance**. In Mendel's law of segregation, the F_1 generation have either purple or white flowers. This is an example of **complete dominance**. **Incomplete dominance** is when the F_1 generation results in an appearance somewhere between the two parents. For example, red flowers crossed with white flowers produce an F_1 generation of pink flowers. The F_1 generation still carries the red and white traits, resulting in an F_2 generation with a phenotypic ratio of 1:2:1. In **codominance,** the genes may form new phenotypes. The ABO blood grouping is an example of codominance. A and B are of equal strength and O is recessive. Therefore, type A blood may have the genotypes of AA or AO, type B blood may have the genotypes of BB or BO, type AB blood has the genotype A and B, and type O blood has two recessive O genes.

Knowledge of pedigree charts

A family pedigree is a collection of a family's history for a particular trait. As you work your way through the pedigree of interest, you apply the Mendelian inheritance theories. In tracing a trait, you map the generations in a pedigree chart, similar to a family tree but with the alleles present. In a case where both parents have a particular trait and one of two children also express this trait, then the trait is due to a dominant allele. In contrast, if both parents do not express a trait and one of their children does, that trait is due to a recessive allele.

Analyzing genetic inheritance problems

The same techniques of pedigree analysis apply when tracing inherited disorders. Thousands of genetic disorders result from a recessive trait. These disorders range from non-lethal traits (such as albinism) to life-threatening (such as cystic fibrosis).

Most people with recessive disorders are born to parents with normal phenotypes. The mating of heterozygous parents would result in an offspring genotypic ratio of 1:2:1; thus 1 out of 4 offspring would express this recessive trait. The heterozygous parents are called carriers because they do not express the trait phenotypically, but can pass the trait on to their offspring.

Lethal dominant alleles are much less common than lethal recessives. This is because lethal dominant alleles are not masked in heterozygotes.

Mutations in a gene of the sperm or egg can result in a lethal dominant allele, usually killing the developing offspring.

Sex-linked traits - The Y chromosome found only in males (XY) carries very little genetic information, whereas the X chromosome found in females (XX) carries very important information. Since men have no second X chromosome to cover up a recessive gene, the recessive trait is expressed more often in men. Women need the recessive gene on both X chromosomes to show the trait. Examples of sex linked traits include hemophilia and color blindness.

Sex-influenced traits – Sex hormones influence some traits. Male pattern baldness is an example of a sex-influenced trait. Testosterone influences the expression of the gene. Thus, men are more susceptible to hair loss.

Nondisjunction - During meiosis, chromosomes fail to separate properly. One sex cell may get both chromosomes and another may get none. Depending on the chromosomes involved this may or may not be serious. Offspring end up with either a missing chromosome or an extra chromosome. An example of nondisjunction is Down syndrome, where three copies of chromosome 21 are present.

Chromosome Theory - Introduced by Walter Sutton in the early 1900's. In the late 1800's, the processes of mitosis and meiosis were explained. Sutton saw how this explanation confirmed Mendel's "factors". The chromosome theory basically states that genes are located on chromosomes that undergo independent assortment and segregation.

0023 Understand the synthesis of DNA, RNA, and protein

Nucleic acids consist of DNA (deoxyribonucleic acid) and RNA (ribonucleic acid).

Nucleic acids contain the code for the amino acid sequence of proteins and the instructions for replicating. The monomer of nucleic acids is a nucleotide. A nucleotide consists of a 5-carbon sugar (deoxyribose in DNA, ribose in RNA), a phosphate group, and a nitrogenous base. The base sequence is the code or the instructions. There are five bases: adenine, thymine, cytosine, guanine, and uracil. Uracil is found only in RNA and replaces thymine. The following provides a summary of nucleic acid structure:

	SUGAR	PHOSPHATE	BASES
DNA	deoxy-ribose	present	adenine, thymine, cytosine, guanine
RNA	ribose	present	adenine, uracil, cytosine, guanine

Due to the molecular structure, adenine will always pair with thymine in DNA or uracil in RNA. Cytosine always pairs with guanine in both DNA and RNA.

This allows for the symmetry of the DNA molecule seen below.

Adenine and thymine (or uracil) are linked by two covalent bonds and cytosine and guanine are linked by three covalent bonds. Guanine and cytosine are harder to break apart than thymine (uracil) and adenine because of the greater number of bonds between the bases. The double-stranded DNA molecule forms a double helix, or twisted ladder, shape.

DNA replication, potential errors, and implications of these errors

DNA replicates semiconservatively. This means the two original strands are conserved and serve as a template for the new strand.

In DNA replication, the first step is to separate the two strands. As they separate, they unwind the supercoils to reduce tension. An enzyme called **helicase** unwinds the DNA as the replication fork proceeds and **topoisomerases** relieve the tension by nicking one strand and relaxing the supercoil.

Once the strands have separated, they must be stabilized. Single-strand binding proteins (SSBs) bind to the single strands until replication is complete.

An RNA polymerase called primase adds ribonucleotides to the DNA template to initiate DNA synthesis. This short RNA-DNA hybrid is called a **primer**. Once the DNA is single stranded, **DNA polymerases** add nucleotides in the 5' → 3' direction.

As DNA synthesis proceeds along the replication fork, it becomes obvious that replication is semi-discontinuous, meaning one strand is synthesized in the direction the replication fork is moving and the other is synthesized in the opposite direction. The continuously synthesized strand is the **leading strand** and the discontinuously synthesized strand is the **lagging strand**. As the replication fork proceeds, new primer is added to the lagging strand and it is synthesized discontinuously in small fragments called **Okazaki fragments**.

The RNA primers that remain must be removed and replaced with deoxyribonucleotides. DNA polymerase has 5' → 3' polymerase activity and has 3' → 5' exonuclease activity. This enzyme binds to the nick between the Okazaki fragment and the RNA primer. It removes the primer and adds deoxyribonucleotides in the 5' → 3' direction. The nick still remains until **DNA ligase** seals it producing the final product, a double-stranded segment of DNA.

Once the double-stranded segment is replicated, there is a proofreading system carried out by DNA replication enzymes. In eukaryotes, DNA polymerases have 3' → 5' exonuclease activity—they move backwards and remove nucleotides where the enzyme recognizes an error, then add the correct nucleotide in the 5' → 3' direction. In E. coli, DNA polymerase II synthesizes DNA during repair of DNA damage.

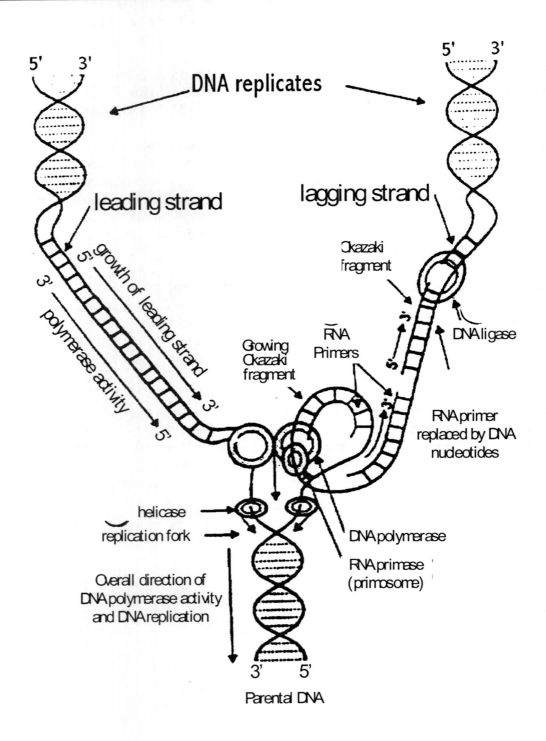

DNA replicates

leading strand

lagging strand

5' 3'

5' 3'

Okazaki fragment

growth of leading strand

polymerase activity

Growing Okazaki fragment

RNA Primers

DNA ligase

RNA primer replaced by DNA nucleotides

helicase

replication fork

DNA polymerase

RNA primase (primosome)

Overall direction of DNA polymerase activity and DNA replication

3' 5'

Parental DNA

Protein synthesis

Proteins are synthesized through the processes of transcription and translation. Three major classes of RNA carry out these processes: messenger RNA (mRNA), ribosomal RNA (rRNA), and transfer RNA (tRNA). **Messenger RNA** contains information for translation. **Ribosomal RNA** is a structural component of the ribosome and **transfer RNA** carries amino acids to the ribosome for protein synthesis.

Transcription is similar in prokaryotes and eukaryotes. During transcription, the DNA molecule is copied into an RNA molecule (mRNA). Transcription occurs through the steps of initiation, elongation, and termination. Transcription also occurs for rRNA and tRNA, but the focus here is on mRNA.

Initiation begins at the promoter of the double-stranded DNA molecule. The promoter is a specific region of DNA that directs the **RNA polymerase** to bind to the DNA. The double-stranded DNA opens up and RNA polymerase begins transcription in the 5' → 3' direction by pairing ribonucleotides to the deoxyribonucleotides as follows to get a complementary mRNA segment:

Deoxyribonucleotide		Ribonucleotide
A	→	U
G	→	C

Elongation is the synthesis on the mRNA strand in the 5' → 3' direction. The new mRNA rapidly separates from the DNA template and the complementary DNA strands pair together.

Termination of transcription occurs at the end of a gene. Cleavage occurs at specific sites on the mRNA. Termination factors aid this process.

In eukaryotes, mRNA goes through **posttranscriptional processing** before going on to translation.
There are three basic steps of processing:

1. **5' capping** – The addition of a base with a methyl attached to it that protects the 5' end from degradation and serves as the site where ribosomes bind to the mRNA for translation.

2. **3' polyadenylation** – The addition of 100-300 adenines to the free 3' end of mRNA resulting in a poly-A-tail.

3. **Intron removal**- The removal of non-coding introns and the splicing together of coding exons to form the mature mRNA.

Translation is the process in which the mRNA sequence becomes a polypeptide. The mRNA sequence determines the amino acid sequence of a protein by following a pattern called the genetic code. The **genetic code** consists of 64 triplet nucleotide combinations called **codons**. Three codons are termination codons and the remaining 61 code for amino acids. mRNA codes for 20 amino acids. Amino acids are the building blocks of protein. They are attached together by peptide bonds to form a polypeptide chain.

Ribosomes are the site of translation. They contain rRNA and many proteins. Translation occurs in three steps: initiation, elongation, and termination. Initiation occurs when the methylated tRNA binds to the ribosome to form a complex. This complex then binds to the 5' cap of the mRNA. In elongation, tRNAs carry the amino acid to the ribosome and place it in order according to the mRNA sequence. tRNA is very specific – it only accepts one of the 20 amino acids that corresponds to the anticodon. The anticodon is complementary to the codon. For example, using the codon sequence below:

the mRNA reads A U G / G A G / C A U / G C U
the anticodons are U A C / C U C / G U A / C G A

Termination occurs when the ribosome reaches any one of the three stop codons: UAA, UAG, or UGA. The newly formed polypeptide then undergoes posttranslational modification to alter or remove portions of the polypeptide.

0024 Understand genes, chromosomes, and changes in genetic material

Chromosomes are cellular structures that carry DNA. **Genes** are regions of chromosomes that are the inheritable units of the genomic sequence, coding for specific traits. Cells have a tightly regulated system of gene expression. Changes in chromosomes and genes can have a variety of effects.

Control of gene expression in cells

In bacterial cells, the *lac* operon is a good example of the control of gene expression. The *lac* operon contains the genes that code for the enzymes used to convert lactose into fuel (glucose and galactose). The *lac* operon contains three genes, *lac Z*, *lac Y*, and *lac A*. *Lac Z* codes for an enzyme that converts lactose into glucose and galactose. *Lac Y* codes for an enzyme that causes lactose to enter the cell. *Lac A* codes for an enzyme that acetylates lactose.

The *lac* operon also contains a promoter and an operator that is the "off and on" switch for the operon. A protein called the repressor switches the operon off when it binds to the operator. When lactose is absent, the repressor is active and the operon is turned off. The operon is turned on again when allolactose (formed from lactose) inactivates the repressor by binding to it.

Mutations in DNA molecules and their effect on protein structure and function

Mutations are inheritable changes in DNA and may result from errors in replication or spontaneous rearrangement of one or more segments by factors like radioactivity, drugs, and chemicals. The severity of the change is not as critical as where the change occurs. DNA contains large segments of non-coding areas called introns. The important coding areas are called exons. If an error occurs in an intron, there is no effect. If the error occurs on an exon, it may be minor to lethal depending on the severity of the mistake. Mutations may occur on somatic or sex cells. Usually the mutations on sex cells are more dangerous since they contain the basis of all information for the developing offspring. However, mutations are not always bad. They are the basis of evolution and if they create a favorable variation that enhances the organism's survival they are beneficial. But mutations may also lead to abnormalities, birth defects, and even death. There are several types of mutations.

A **point mutation** is a mutation involving a single nucleotide or a few adjacent nucleotides. Let's suppose a normal sequence was as follows:

Normal:	A B C D E F
Duplication - one nucleotide is repeated	A B **C C** D E F
Inversion - a segment of the sequence is flipped around	A **E D C B** F
Deletion - a nucleotide is left out	A B C E F
	(D is lost)
Insertion or **Translocation** - a segment from another place on the DNA is stuck in the wrong place	A B C **R S** D E F
Breakage - a piece is lost	A B C (DEF is lost)

Deletion and insertion mutations that shift the reading frame are **frame shift mutations**.

A **silent mutation** makes no change in the amino acid sequence, therefore it does not alter the protein function. A **missense mutation** results in an alteration in the amino acid sequence. A mutation's effect on protein function depends on which amino acids are involved and how many are involved. The structure of a protein usually determines its function. A mutation that does not alter the structure will probably have little or no effect on the protein's function. However, a mutation that does alter the structure of a protein and can severely affect protein activity is called a **loss-of-function mutation**. Sickle-cell anemia and cystic fibrosis are examples of loss-of-function mutations.

Sickle-cell anemia is characterized by weakness, heart failure, joint and muscular impairment, fatigue, abdominal pain and dysfunction, impaired mental function, and eventual death. The mutation that causes this genetic disorder is a point mutation in the sixth amino acid of hemoglobin. A normal hemoglobin molecule has glutamic acid as the sixth amino acid and the sickle-cell hemoglobin has valine at the sixth position. This mutation causes the chemical properties of hemoglobin to change. The hemoglobin of a sickle-cell person has a lower affinity for oxygen, causing red blood cells to have a sickle shape. The sickle shape of the red blood cell causes the formatin of clogs because the cells do not pass through capillaries well.

Cystic fibrosis is the most common genetic disorder of people with European ancestry. This disorder affects the exocrine system. A fibrous cyst is formed on the pancreas that blocks the pancreatic ducts. This causes sweat glands to release high levels of salt. Mucous glands secrete a thick mucous that accumulates in the lungs. This accumulation of mucous causes bacterial infections and possible death. Cystic fibrosis cannot be cured, but can be treated for a short while. Most children with the disorder die before adulthood. Scientists identified a protein that transports chloride ions across cell membranes. Those with cystic fibrosis have a mutation in the gene coding for this protein. The majority of the mutant alleles have a deletion of the three nucleotides coding for phenylalanine at position 508. Other people with the disorder have mutant alleles caused by substitution, deletion, and frameshift mutations.

Analyze the techniques used to screen for genetic disorders

Some genetic disorders can be prevented. The parents can be screened for genetic disorders before the child is conceived or in the early stages of pregnancy. Genetic counselors determine the risk of producing offspring that may express a genetic disorder. The counselor reviews the family's pedigree and determines the frequency of a recessive allele. While genetic counseling is helpful for future parents, there is no certainty in the outcome.

There are some genetic disorders that can be discovered in a heterozygous parent. For example, genetic testing can uncover sickle-cell anemia and cystic fibrosis alleles in carriers. If the parents are carriers but decide to have children anyway, fetal testing is available during the pregnancy. There are a few techniques available to determine if a developing fetus will have the genetic disorder.

Amniocentesis is a procedure in which a needle is inserted into the uterus to extract some of the amniotic fluid surrounding the fetus. Some disorders can be detected by chemicals in the fluid. Other disorders can be detected by karyotyping cells cultured from the fluid to identify certain chromosomal defects.

A physician removes some of the fetal tissue from the placenta in a technique called **chorionic villus sampling (CVS)**. The cells are then karyotyped as they are in amniocentesis. The advantage of CVS is that the cells can be karyotyped immediately, unlike in amniocentesis which take several weeks to culture.

Unlike amniocentesis and CVS, **ultrasounds** are a non-invasive technique for detecting genetic disorders. Ultrasound can only detect physical abnormalities of the fetus.

Newborn screening is now routinely performed in the United States at birth. Phenylketonuria (PKU) is a recessively inherited disorder that does not allow children to properly break down the amino acid phenylalanine. This amino acid and its by-product accumulate in the blood to toxic levels, resulting in mental retardation. This can be prevented by screening at birth for this defect and treating it with a special diet.

Understand the role of nonnuclear inheritance

Mitochondrial DNA is passed to the next generation by the mother. A genetic defect in the mother's mitochondrial DNA will pass to her offspring, regardless of the paternal DNA.

Understand the role of genetic engineering in the medical field

Genetic engineering has made enormous contributions to medicine and has opened the door to DNA technology.
The use of DNA probes and the polymerase chain reaction (PCR) has enabled scientists to identify and detect elusive pathogens. Diagnosis of genetic disease is now possible before the onset of symptoms.

Genetic engineering has allowed for the treatment of some genetic disorders. **Gene therapy** is the introduction of a normal allele to the somatic cells to replace the defective allele. The medical field has had success in treating patients with a single enzyme deficiency disease. Gene therapy has allowed doctors and scientists to introduce a normal allele that provides the missing enzyme.

Insulin and mammalian growth hormones have been produced in bacteria by gene-splicing techniques. Insulin treatment helps control diabetes for millions of people who suffer from the disease. The insulin produced in genetically engineered bacteria is chemically identical to that made in the pancreas. Human growth hormone (HGH) has been genetically engineered for treatment of dwarfism caused by insufficient amounts of HGH. HGH is being further researched for treatment of broken bones and severe burns.

Biotechnology has advanced the techniques used to create vaccines. Genetic engineering allows for the modification of a pathogen in order to attenuate it for vaccine use. In fact, vaccines created by a pathogen attenuated by gene-splicing may be safer than those that use the traditional mutants.

Forensic scientists regularly use DNA technology to solve crimes. DNA testing can determine a person's guilt or innocence. A suspect's DNA fingerprint is compared to the DNA found at the crime scene. A fingerprints match can establish guilt.

Understand the role of genetic engineering in the agricultural and environmental fields

Many microorganisms are used to detoxify toxic chemicals and to recycle waste. Sewage treatment plants use microbes to degrade organic compounds. Some compounds, like chlorinated hydrocarbons, cannot be easily degraded. Scientists are working on ways to genetically modify microbes to allow them to degrade the harmful compounds that the current microbes cannot.

Genetic engineering has also benefited agriculture. For example, many dairy cows are given bovine growth hormone to increase milk production. Commercially grown plants are often genetically modified for optimal growth.

Strains of wheat, cotton, and soybeans have been developed to resist herbicides used to control weeds. This allows for the successful growth of the plants while destroying the weeds. Crop plants are also being engineered to resist infections and pests. Scientists can genetically modify crops to contain a viral gene that does not affect the plant and will "vaccinate" the plant from a virus attack. Crop plants are now being modified to resist insect attacks. This allows farmers to reduce the amount of pesticide used on plants.

Knowledge of genetic engineering techniques

In its simplest form, genetic engineering requires enzymes to cut DNA, a vector, and a host organism for the recombinant DNA. A **restriction enzyme** is a bacterial enzyme that cuts foreign DNA in specific locations. The restriction fragment that results can be inserted into a bacterial plasmid **(vector)**. Other vectors that may be used include viruses and bacteriophages. The splicing of restriction fragments into a plasmid results in a recombinant plasmid. This recombinant plasmid can then be placed in a host cell, usually a bacterial cell, for replication.

The use of recombinant DNA provides a means to transplant genes among species. This opens the door for cloning specific genes of interest. Hybridization can be used to find a gene of interest. A probe is a molecule complementary in sequence to the gene of interest. The probe, once it has bonded to the gene, can be detected by labeling with a radioactive isotope or a fluorescent tag.

Gel electrophoresis is another method for analyzing DNA. Electrophoresis separates DNA or protein by size or electrical charge. The DNA runs towards the positive charge and the DNA fragments separate by size. The gel is treated with a DNA-binding dye that fluoresces under ultraviolet light. A picture of the gel can be taken and used for analysis.

One of the most widely used genetic engineering techniques is the **polymerase chain reaction (PCR)**. PCR is a technique in which a piece of DNA can be amplified into billions of copies within a few hours. This process requires a primer to specify the segment to be copied, and an enzyme (usually taq polymerase) to amplify the DNA. PCR has allowed scientists to perform multiple procedures on small amounts of DNA.

Understand the ethical, legal, and social implications of genetic engineering

Genetic engineering has drastically advanced with biotechnology. With these advancements come concerns about safety and ethics. Strict government regulations have addressed many safety concerns. The FDA, USDA, EPA, and National Institutes of Health are just a few of the government agencies that regulate pharmaceutical, food, and environmental technology advancements.

Several ethical questions arise when discussing biotechnology. Should embryonic stem cell research be allowed? Is animal testing humane? There are strong arguments for both sides of the issues and there are some government regulations in place to monitor these issues.

0025 Analyze the process of natural selection

Analyze the role of natural selection on evolution

Natural selection is based on the survival of certain traits in a population through the course of time.   The phrase "survival of the fittest" is often associated with natural selection. Fitness is the contribution an individual makes to the gene pool of the next generation.

Natural selection acts on phenotypes. An organism's phenotype is constantly exposed to its environment. Based on an organism's phenotype, selection indirectly adapts a population to its environment by maintaining favorable genotypes in the gene pool.

There are three modes of natural selection. **Stabilizing selection** favors the more common phenotypes, **directional selection** shifts the frequency of phenotypes in one direction, and **diversifying selection** favors individuals on both extremes of the phenotypic range.

Sexual selection leads to the secondary sex characteristics of males and females. Animals that use mating behaviors may be successful or unsuccessful. A male animal that lacks attractive plumage or has a weak mating call will not attract females, thereby eventually limiting that gene in the gene pool. Mechanical isolation, where sex organs do not fit the female, has an obvious disadvantage.

Recognize the relationship between phenotype and its selective advantage in the environment

The environment can have an impact on phenotype. For example, a person living at a higher altitude will have a different amount of red and white blood cells than a person living at sea level.

In some cases, a particular trait is advantageous to the organism in a particular environment. Sickle-cell disease causes a low oxygen level in the blood which results in red blood cells having a sickle shape. About one in every ten African-Americans have the sickle-cell trait. These heterozygous carriers are usually healthy compared to homozygous individuals who can suffer severe detrimental effects. In the tropical Africa environment, heterozygotes are more resistant to malaria than those who do not carry any copies of the sickle-cell gene.

Sources of variation in a population

Heritable variation is responsible for the individuality of organisms. An individual's phenotype is based on inherited genotype and the surrounding environment. Mutation and sexual recombination creates genetic variation. Mutations may be errors in replication or spontaneous rearrangements of one or more segments of DNA.

Mutations contribute a minimal amount of variation in a population. It is the unique **recombination** of existing alleles that causes the majority of genetic differences. Recombination is caused by the crossing over of the parent genes during meiosis. This results in unique offspring. With all the possible mating combinations in the world, it is obvious that sexual reproduction is the primary cause of genetic variation.

Recognize the factors that lead to speciation

The most commonly used species concept is the **Biological Species Concept (BSC)**.

This concept states that a species is a reproductive community of populations that occupy a specific niche in nature. It focuses on reproductive isolation of populations as the primary criterion for recognition of species status. The biological species concept does not apply to organisms that are asexual in their reproduction, fossil organisms, or distinctive populations that hybridize.

Reproductive isolation is caused by any factor that impedes two species from producing viable, fertile hybrids. Reproductive barriers can be categorized as **prezygotic** (premating) or **postzygotic** (postmating).

The prezygotic barriers include:

1. Habitat isolation – species occupy different habitats in the same territory.
2. Temporal isolation – populations reaching sexual maturity/flowering at different times of the year.
3. Ethological isolation – behavioral differences that reduce or prevent interbreeding between individuals of different species (including pheromones and other attractants).
4. Mechanical isolation – structural differences that make gamete transfer difficult or impossible.
5. Gametic isolation – male and female gametes do not attract each other; no fertilization.

The postzygotic barriers include:

1. Hybrid inviability – hybrids die before sexual maturity.
2. Hybrid sterility – disrupts gamete formation; no normal sex cells.
3. Hybrid breakdown – reduces viability or fertility in progeny of the F_2 backcross.

Geographical isolation can also lead to the origin of species. **Allopatric speciation** is speciation without geographic overlap. It is the accumulation of genetic differences through division of a species' range, either through a physical barrier separating the population or through expansion by dispersal. In **sympatric speciation**, new species arise within the range of parent populations. Populations are sympatric if their geographical range overlaps. This usually involves the rapid accumulation of genetic differences (usually chromosomal rearrangements) that prevent interbreeding with adjacent populations.

0026   Analyze the theory of evolution

Compare alternative mechanisms of evolution

There are two theories on the rate of evolution. **Gradualism** is the theory that minor evolutionary changes occur at a regular rate. Darwin's book, "On the Origin of Species," is based on this theory of gradualism.

Charles Darwin was born in 1809 and spent 5 years in his twenties on a ship called the *Beagle*. Of all the locations the *Beagle* sailed to, it was the Galapagos Islands that infatuated Darwin. There he collected 13 species of finches that were quite similar. He could not accurately determine whether these finches were of the same species. He later learned these finches were in fact separate species. Darwin began to hypothesize that a new species arose from its ancestors by the gradual collection of adaptations to a different environment. Darwin's most popular hypothesis involves the beak size of Galapagos finches. He theorized that the finches' beak sizes evolved to accommodate different food sources. Many people did not believe in Darwin's theories until recent field studies proved successful.

Although Darwin believed the origin of species was gradual, he was bewildered by the gaps in fossil records of living organisms. **Punctuated equilibrium** is the model of evolution that states that organismal form diverges and species form rapidly over relatively short periods of geological history and then progress through long stages of stasis with little or no change. Punctuationalists use fossil records to support their claim. It is probable that both gradualism and punctuated equilibrium are correct, depending on the particular lineage studied.

Analyze the conditions that affect the gene pool

Evolution currently is defined as a change in genotype over time. Gene frequencies shift and change from generation to generation. Populations evolve, not individuals. The **Hardy-Weinberg** theory of gene equilibrium is a mathematical prediction to show shifting gene patterns. Let's use the letter "*A*" to represent the dominant condition of normal skin pigment, and the letter "*a*" to represent the recessive condition of albinism. In a population, there are three possible genotypes: *AA, Aa,* and *aa. AA* and *Aa* individuals would have normal skin pigment and only *aa* individuals would be albinos.

According to the Hardy-Weinberg law, there are five requirements that keep gene frequency stable and limit evolution:
1.   There is no mutation in the population.
2.   There are no selection pressures; one gene is not more desirable in the environment.
3.   There is no mating preference; mating is random.
4.   The population is isolated; there is no immigration or emigration.
5.   The population is large (mathematical probability is more accurate with a large sample).

The above conditions are extremely difficult to meet. If these five conditions are not met, then gene frequency can shift, leading to evolution. Let's say in a population, 75% of the population has normal skin pigment (*AA* and *Aa*) and 25% are albino (*aa*). Using the following formula, we can determine the frequency of the *A* allele and the *a* allele in a population.

This formula can be used over generations to determine if evolution is occurring. The formula is: $1 = p^2 + 2pq + q^2$; where 1 is the total population, p^2 is the number of *AA* individuals, $2pq$ is the number of *Aa* individuals, and q^2 is the number of *aa* individuals.

Since you cannot tell by looking if an individual is *AA* or *Aa*, you must use the *aa* individuals to find that frequency first. As stated above *aa* was 25% of the population. Since $aa = q^2$, we can determine the value of q (or a) by finding the square root of 0.25, which is 0.5. Therefore, 0.5 of the population has the *a* gene. In order to find the value for p, use the following formula: $1 = p + q$. This would make the value of $p = 0.5$.

The gene pool is all the alleles at all gene loci in all individuals of a population. The Hardy-Weinberg theorem describes the gene pool in a non-evolving population. It states that the frequencies of alleles and genotypes in a population's gene pool are random unless acted on by something other than sexual recombination.

Now, to find the number of *AA*, plug it into the first formula:

$$AA = p^2 = 0.5 \times 0.5 = 0.25$$
$$Aa = 2pq = 2(0.5 \times 0.5) = 0.5$$
$$aa = q^2 = 0.5 \times 0.5 = 0.25$$

Any problem you may have with Hardy-Weinberg will have an obvious squared number. The square of that number will be the frequency of the recessive gene, and you can figure anything else out knowing the formula and the frequency of q.

When frequencies vary from the Hardy-Weinberg equilibrium, the population is evolving. The change to the gene pool is on such a small scale that it is called microevolution. Certain factors increase the chances of variability in a population, thus leading to evolution. Items that increase variability include mutations, sexual reproduction, immigration, large population, and variation in geographic local. Changes that decrease variation are natural selection, emigration, small population, and random mating.

Knowledge of the theories of the origin of life

The hypothesis that life developed on Earth from nonliving materials is the most widely accepted theory. The transformation from nonliving materials to life had four stages. The first stage was the nonliving (abiotic) synthesis of small monomers such as amino acids and nucleotides. In the second stage, these monomers combine to form polymers, such as proteins and nucleic acids. The third stage was the accumulation of these polymers into droplets called protobionts. The last stage was the origin of heredity, with RNA as the first genetic material.

The first stage of this theory was hypothesized in the 1920s. A. I. Oparin and J. B. S. Haldane were the first to theorize that the primitive atmosphere was a reducing atmosphere with no oxygen present. The gases were rich in hydrogen, methane, water, and ammonia. In the 1950s, Stanley Miller proved Oparin's theory in the laboratory by combining the above gases. When given an electrical spark, he was able to synthesize simple amino acids. It is commonly accepted that amino acids appeared before DNA. Other laboratory experiments have supported that the other stages in the origin of life theory could have happened.

Other scientists believe simpler hereditary systems originated before nucleic acids. In 1991, Julius Rebek was able to synthesize a simple organic molecule that replicates itself. According to his theory, this simple molecule may be the precursor of RNA.

Analyze the progression of life forms

Prokaryotes are the simplest life form. Their small genome size limits the number of genes that control metabolic activities. Over time, some prokaryotic groups became multicellular organisms for this reason. Prokaryotes then evolved to form complex bacterial communities where species benefit from one another.

The **endosymbiotic theory** of the origin of eukaryotes states that eukaryotes arose from symbiotic groups of prokaryotic cells. According to this theory, smaller prokaryotes lived within larger prokaryotic cells, eventually evolving into chloroplasts and mitochondria.

Chloroplasts are the descendant of photosynthetic prokaryotes and mitochondria are likely the descendants of bacteria that were aerobic heterotrophs. Serial endosymbiosis is a sequence of endosymbiotic events. Serial endosymbiosis may also play a role in the progression of life forms to become eukaryotes.

Understand the importance of geological and fossil records in determining evolution

Fossils are the key to understanding biological history. They are the preserved remnants left by an organism that lived in the past. Scientists have established the geological time scale to determine the age of a fossil. The geological time scale is broken down into four eras: the Precambrian, Paleozoic, Mesozoic, and Cenozoic. The eras are further broken down into periods that represent a distinct age in the history of the Earth and its life. Scientists use rock layers called strata to date fossils. The older layers of rock are at the bottom. This allows scientists to correlate the rock layers with the era they date back to. Radiometric dating is a more precise method of dating fossils. Rocks and fossils contain isotopes of elements accumulated over time. The isotope's half-life is used to date older fossils by determining the amount of isotope remaining and comparing it to the half-life.

Dating fossils is helpful in the construction of evolutionary trees. Scientists can arrange the succession of animals based on their fossil record. The fossils of an animal's ancestors can be dated and placed on its evolutionary tree. For example, the branched evolution of horses shows that the modern horse's ancestors were larger, had a reduced number of toes, and had teeth modified for grazing.

Subarea VI. Matter and Energy in Ecosystems

0027 Understand populations and communities

Factors that affect population size and growth rate

A **population** is a group of individuals of one species that live in the same general area. Many factors can affect population size and population growth rate. Population size can depend on the total amount of life a habitat can support. This is the carrying capacity of the environment. Once the habitat runs out of food, water, shelter, or space, the carrying capacity decreases, and then stabilizes.

Limiting factors can affect population growth. As a population increases, the competition for resources is more intense, and the growth rate declines. This is a **density-dependent** growth factor. The carrying capacity can be determined by the density-dependent factor. **Density-independent factors** affect the individuals regardless of population size. The weather and climate are good examples. Too hot or too cold temperatures may kill many individuals from a population that has not reached its carrying capacity.

Population growth curves

Zero population growth rate occurs when the birth and death rates are equal in a population. Exponential growth rate occurs when there is an abundance of resources and the growth rate is at its maximum, called the intrinsic rate of increase. This relationship can be understood in a growth curve.

An exponentially growing population starts off with little change, then rapidly increases.

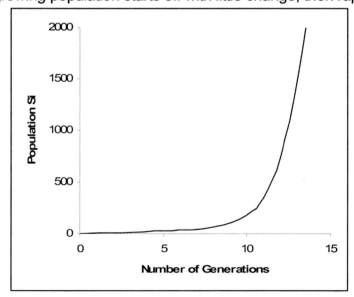

Logistic population growth incorporates the carrying capacity into the growth rate. As a population reaches the carrying capacity, the growth rate begins to slow down and level off.

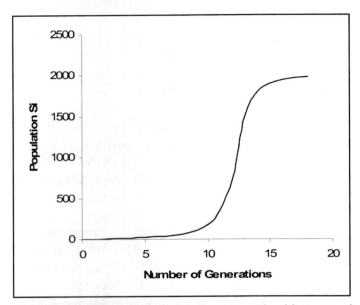

Many populations follow this model of population growth. Humans, however, are an exponentially growing population. Eventually, the carrying capacity of the Earth will be reached, and the growth rate will level off. How and when this will occur remains a mystery.

Relationships among organisms in a community

There are many interactions that may occur between different species living together. Predation, parasitism, competition, commensalism, and mutualism are the different types of relationships populations have with each other.

Predation and **parasitism** result in a benefit for one species and a detriment for the other. Predation is when a predator eats its prey. The most common conception of predation is of a carnivore consuming other animals. Although not always resulting in the death of the plant, herbivory is another form of predation. Parasitism involves a predator that lives on or in its host, causing detrimental effects to the host. Insects and viruses living off and reproducing in their hosts is an example of parasitism. Many plants and animals have defenses against predators. Some plants have poisonous chemicals that will harm the predator if ingested and some animals are camouflaged so they are harder to detect.

Competition is when two or more species in a community use the same resources. Competition is usually detrimental to both populations. Competition is often difficult to find in nature because competition between two populations is not continuous. Either the weaker population will cease to exist, or one population will evolve to utilize other available resources.

Symbiosis is when two species live close together. Parasitism is one example of symbiosis described above. Another example of symbiosis is commensalism. **Commensalism** occurs when one species benefits from the other without harmful effects. **Mutualism** is when both species benefit from the other. Species involved in mutualistic relationships must coevolve to survive. As one species evolves, the other must as well if it is to be successful in life. The grouper fish and a species of shrimp live in a mutualistic relationship. The shrimp feed off parasites living on the grouper. Thus, the shrimp are fed and the grouper stays healthy. Many microorganisms exist in mutualistic relationships.

Effects of population density on the environment

Population density is the number of individuals per unit area or volume. The spacing pattern of individuals in an area is dispersion. **Dispersion patterns** can be clumped, with individuals grouped in patches; uniform, where individuals are approximately equidistant from each other; or random.

Population densities are usually estimated based on a few representative plots. Aggregation of a population in a relatively small geographic area can have detrimental effects on the environment. Food, water, and other resources will be rapidly consumed, resulting in an unstable environment. A low population density is less harmful to the environment. The use of natural resources will be more dispersed, allowing for the environment to recover and continue growth.

0028 Understand types and characteristics of ecosystems and biomes and factors affecting their change over time

Flow of energy through trophic levels of an ecosystem

Trophic levels are based on the feeding relationships that determine energy flow and chemical cycling.

Autotrophs are the primary producers of the ecosystem. **Producers** mainly consist of plants. **Primary consumers** are the next trophic level. The primary consumers are the herbivores that eat plants or algae. **Secondary consumers** are the carnivores that eat the primary consumers. **Tertiary consumers** eat the secondary consumer. These trophic levels may go higher depending on the ecosystem. **Decomposers** are consumers that feed off animal waste and dead organisms. This pathway of food transfer is the food chain.

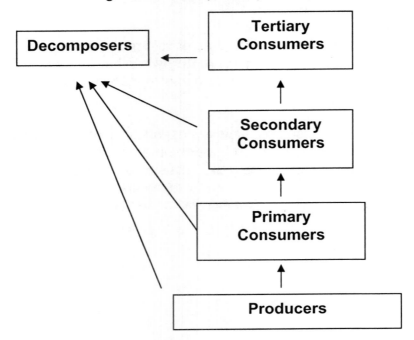

Most food chains are more elaborate, becoming food webs.

Pyramid models

Energy is lost as the trophic levels progress from producer to tertiary consumer. The amount of energy that is transferred between trophic levels is called the ecological efficiency. The visual of this energy flow is represented in a **pyramid of productivity**.

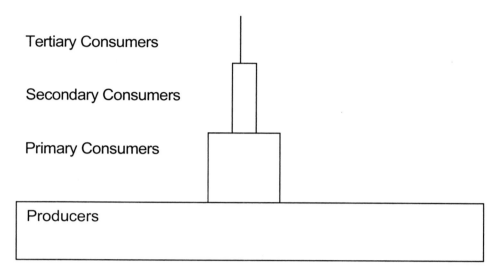

Tertiary Consumers

Secondary Consumers

Primary Consumers

Producers

The **biomass pyramid** represents the total dry weight of organisms in each trophic level. A **pyramid of numbers** is a representation of the population size of each trophic level. The producers, being the most populous, are on the bottom of this pyramid with the tertiary consumers on the top with the fewest numbers.

Ecological succession and biotic and abiotic factors

Succession is an orderly process of replacing a community that has been damaged or has begun where no life previously existed. Primary succession occurs where life never existed before, as in a flooded area or a new volcanic island. Secondary succession takes place in communities that were once flourishing but were disturbed by some source, either man or nature, but not totally stripped. A climax community is a community that is established and flourishing.

Abiotic and biotic factors play a role in succession. **Biotic factors** are living things in an ecosystem (e.g., plants, animals, bacteria, and fungi). **Abiotic factors** are non-living aspects of an ecosystem (e.g., soil quality, rainfall, and temperature).

Abiotic factors affect succession by way of the species that colonize the area. Certain species will or will not survive depending on the weather, climate, or soil make-up. Biotic factors such as inhibition of one species due to another may occur. This may be due to some form of competition between the species.

Geographic distributions of major biomes

An ecosystem includes all living things in a specific area and the non-living things that affect them. The term **biome** is usually used to classify the general types of ecosystems in the world. Each biome contains distinctive organisms best adapted to that natural environment (including geological make-up, latitude, and altitude). All the living things in a biome are naturally in equilibrium and disturbances in any one element may cause upset throughout the system. It should be noted that these biomes may have various names in different areas. For example steppe, savanna, veld, prairie, outback, and scrub are all regional terms that describe the same biome, grassland.

The major terrestrial biomes are desert, grassland, tundra, boreal forest, tropical rainforest, and temperate forest.

Desert

Deserts exist in any location that receives less that 50 cm of precipitation a year. Despite their lack of water and often desolate appearance, the soils, though loose and silty, tend to be rich and specialized plants and animals do populate deserts. Plant species include xerophytes and succulents. Animals tend to be non-mammalian and small (e.g., lizards and snakes). Large animals are not able to find sufficient shade in the desert and mammals, in general, are not well adapted to storing water and withstanding heat. Deserts may be either hot and dry or cold. Hot and dry deserts are what we typically envision when we think of a desert and occur throughout the world. Hot deserts are located in northern Africa, southwestern United States, and the Middle East. Cold deserts have similarly little vegetation and small animals and are located exclusively near the poles in Antarctica, Greenland, much of central Asia, and the Arctic. Both types of deserts do receive precipitation in the winter, though it is in the form of rain in hot deserts and the form of snow in the cold.

Grassland

As the name suggests, grasslands include large expanses of grass with only a few shrubs or trees. There are both tropical and temperate grasslands.

Tropical grasslands cover much of Australia, South America, and India. The weather is warm year-round with moderate rainfall. However, the rainfall is concentrated in half the year and drought and fires are common in the other half of the year. These fires serve to renew rather than destroy areas within tropical grasslands. This type of grassland supports a large variety of animals from insects to mammals both large and small such as squirrels, mice, gophers, giraffes, zebras, kangaroos, lions, and elephants.

Temperate grasslands receive even less rain than tropical grasslands and are found in South Africa, Eastern Europe, and the western United States. As in tropical grasslands, periods of draught and fire serve to renew the ecosystem. Differences in temperature also differentiate the temperate from the tropical grasslands. Temperate grasslands are cooler in general and experience even colder temperatures in winter. These grasslands support similar types of animals as the tropical grasslands: prairie dogs, deer, mice, coyotes, hawks, snakes, and foxes.

The savanna is grassland with scattered individual trees. Plants of the savanna include shrubs and grasses. Temperatures range from 0 - 25 degrees C in the savanna depending on its location. Rainfall is from 90 to 150 cm per year. The savanna is a transitional biome between the rain forest and the desert that is located in central South America, southern Africa, and parts of Australia.

Tundra

Tundras are treeless plains with extremely low temperatures (-28 to 15 degrees C) and little vegetation or precipitation. Rainfall is limited, ranging from 10 to 15 cm per year. A layer of permanently frozen subsoil, called permafrost, is found in the tundra. The permafrost means that no vegetation with deep root systems can exist in the tundra, but low shrubs, mosses, grasses, and lichen are able to survive. These plants grow low and close together to resist the cold temperature and strong winds. The few animals that live in the tundra are adapted to the cold winters (via layers of subcutaneous fat, hibernation, or migration) and raise their young quickly during the summers. Such species include lemmings, caribou, arctic squirrels and foxes, polar bears, cod, salmon, mosquitoes, falcons, and snow birds.

Both arctic and alpine tundra exist, though their characteristics are extremely similar and are distinguished mainly by the location (arctic tundra is located near the North Pole, while alpine tundra is found in the world's highest mountains).

Polar tundra or Permafrost temperature ranges from -40 to 0 degrees C. It rarely gets above freezing. Rainfall is below 10 cm per year. Most water is bound up as ice. Life is limited.

Forests

There are three types of forests, all characterized by the abundant growth of trees, but with difference in climate, flora, and fauna.

Boreal forest (taiga)

These forests are located near the poles throughout northern Europe, Asia, and North America. The climate typically consists of short, rainy summers followed by long, cold winters with snow. The trees in boreal forests are adapted to the cold winters and are typically evergreens including pine, fir, and spruce. The trees are so thick that there is little undergrowth. A number of animals are adapted to life in the boreal forest, including many mammals such as bear, moose, wolves, chipmunks, weasels, mink, and deer. These coniferous forests have temperatures ranging from -24 to 22 degrees C. Rainfall is between 35 to 40 cm per year. This is the largest terrestrial biome.

Tropical rainforest

Tropical rainforests are located near the equator and are typically warm and wet throughout the entire year. The temperature is constant (25 degrees C) and the length of daylight is about 12 hours. The precipitation is frequent and occurs evenly during the year. In a tropical rainforest, rainfall exceeds 200 cm per year. Tropical rainforests have abundant, diverse species of plants and animals. A tropical dry forest gets scarce rainfall and a tropical deciduous forest has wet and dry seasons. The soil is surprisingly nutrient-poor and most of the biomass is located within the trees themselves. The vegetation is highly diverse including many trees with shallow roots, orchids, vines, ferns, mosses, and palms. Animals are similarly plentiful and varied and include all type of birds, reptiles, bats, insects, and small to medium sized mammals.

Temperate forest

These forests have well defined winters and summers with precipitation throughout the year. Temperate forests are common in western Europe, eastern North America, and parts of Asia. Common trees include deciduous species such as oak, beech, maple, and hickory. Unlike the boreal forests, the canopy in the temperate forest is not particularly heavy and so various smaller plants occupy the understory. Mammals and birds are the predominate form of animal life. Typical species include squirrels, rabbits, skunks, deer, bobcats, and bear. The temperature here range from -24 to 38 degrees C. Rainfall is between 65 and 150 cm per year.

A subtype of temperate forests are Chaparral forests. Chaparral forests experience mild, rainy winters and hot, dry summers. Trees do not grow as well here. Spiny shrubs dominate. Regions include the Mediterranean, the California coastline, and southwestern Australia.

Aquatic ecosystems

Aquatic ecosystems are ecosystems located within bodies of water. Aquatic biomes are divided between fresh water and marine. Freshwater ecosystems are closely linked to terrestrial biomes. Lakes, ponds, rivers, streams, and swamplands are examples of freshwater biomes. Marine areas cover 75% of the earth. This biome is organized by the depth of the water. The intertidal zone is from the tide line to the edge of the water. The littoral zone is from the water's edge to the open sea. It includes coral reef habitats and is the most densely populated area of the marine biome. The open sea zone is divided into the epipelagic zone and the pelagic zone. The epipelagic zone receives more sunlight and has a larger number of species.

The ocean floor is called the benthic zone and is populated with bottom feeders. Marine biomes include coral reefs, estuaries, and several systems within the oceans.

Oceans

Within the world's oceans, there are several separate zones, each with its own temperature profiles and unique species. These zones include intertidal, pelagic, benthic, and abyssal. The interdidal and pelagic zones are further distinguished by the latitude at which they occur. The intertidal zone is the shore area, which is alternately under and above the water, depending on the tides. Algae, mollusks, snails, crabs, and seaweed are all found in the intertidal zones. The pelagic zone is further from land but near the surface of the ocean. This zone is sometimes called the euphotic zone. Temperatures are much cooler than in the intertidal zone and organisms in this zone include surface seaweeds, plankton, various fish, whales, and dolphins. Further below the ocean's surface is the benthic zone, which is even colder and darker. Much seaweed is found in this zone, as well as bacteria, fungi, sponges, anemones, sea stars, and some fish. Deeper still is the abyssal zone, which is the coldest and darkest area of the ocean and has high pressure and low oxygen content. Thermal vents found in the abyssal zone support chemosyntheic bacteria, which are in turn eaten by invertebrates and fishes.

Coral reefs

Coral reefs are located in warm, shallow water near large land masses. The best known example is the Great Barrier Reef off the coast of Australia. The coral itself is the predominant life form in the reefs and obtains its nutrients largely through photosynthesis (performed by the algae). Many other animal life forms also populate coral reefs: many species of fish, octopuses, sea stars, and urchins.

Estuaries

Estuaries are found where fresh and seawater meet. For example, where rivers flow into the oceans. Many species have evolved to thrive in the unique salt concentrations that exist in estuaries. The species include marsh grasses, mangrove trees, oysters, crabs, and certain waterfowl.

Ponds and Lakes

As with the other aquatic biomes, many varied ecosystems occur in ponds and lakes. This is not surprising since lakes vary in size and location. Some lakes are even seasonal, lasting just a few months each year. Additionally, within lakes there are zones, comparable to those in oceans. The littoral zone, located near the shore and at the top of the lake, is the warmest and lightest zone. Organisms in this zone typically include aquatic plants and insects, snails, clams, fish, and amphibians. Further from land, but still at the surface of the lake is the limnetic zone.

Plankton is abundant in the limnetic zone and it is at the bottom of the food chain in this zone, ultimately supporting freshwater fish of all sizes. Deeper in the lake is the profundal zone, which is cooler and darker. Plankton also serves as a valuable food source in this zone since much of it dies and falls to the bottom of the lake. Again, small fish eat this plankton and begin the food chain.

Rivers and Streams

This biome includes moving bodies of water. As expected, the organisms found within streams vary according to latitude and geological features. Additionally, characteristics of the stream change as it flows from its headwaters to the sea. Also, as the depth of rivers increases, zones similar to those seen in the ocean are seen. That is, different species live in the upper, sunlit areas (e.g., algae, top feeding fish, and aquatic insects) and in the darker, bottom areas (e.g., catfish, carp, and microbes).

Wetlands

Wetlands are the only aquatic biome that is partially land-based. They are areas of standing water in which aquatic plants grow. These species, called hydrophytes are adapted to extremely humid and moist conditions and include lilies, cattails, sedges, cypress, and black spruce. Animal life in wetlands includes insects, amphibians, reptiles, many birds, and a few small mammals. Though wetlands are usually classified as a freshwater biome, they are in fact salt marshes that support shrimp, various fish, and grasses.

Effects of biome degradation and destruction on biosphere stability

Humans are continuously searching for new places to form communities. This encroachment on the environment leads to the destruction of wildlife communities.

Conservationists focus on endangered species, but the primary focus should be on protecting the entire biome. If a biome becomes extinct, the wildlife dies or invades another biome.

Preservations established by the government aim at protecting small parts of biomes. While beneficial in the conservation of a few areas, the majority of the environment is still unprotected.

0029   Analyze the cycling of materials through an ecosystem

Processes involved in material cycles

Biogeochemical cycles are nutrient cycles that involve both biotic and abiotic factors.

Water cycle - Two percent of all the available water is fixed and unavailable in ice or the bodies of organisms. Available water includes surface water (e.g., lakes, oceans, rivers) and ground water (e.g., aquifers, wells). 96% of all available water is from ground water. The water cycle is driven by solar energy. Water is recycled through the processes of evaporation and precipitation.

Carbon cycle - Ten percent of all available carbon in the air (in the form of carbon dioxide gas) is fixed by photosynthesis. Plants fix carbon in the form of glucose. Animals eat the plants and are able to obtain carbon. When animals release carbon dioxide through respiration, the plants again have a source of carbon for further fixation.

Nitrogen cycle - Eighty percent of the atmosphere is in the form of nitrogen gas. Nitrogen must be fixed and taken out of the gaseous form to be incorporated into an organism. Only a few genera of bacteria have the correct enzymes to break the triple bond between nitrogen atoms in a process called nitrogen fixation. These bacteria live within the roots of legumes (e.g., peas, beans, alfalfa) and add nitrogen to the soil so it may be taken up by the plant. Nitrogen is necessary to make amino acids and the nitrogenous bases of DNA.

Phosphorus cycle - Phosphorus exists as a mineral and is not found in the atmosphere. Fungi and plant roots have a structure called mycorrhizae that are able to fix insoluble phosphates into usable phosphorus. Urine and decayed matter return phosphorus to the earth where it can be fixed in the plant. Phosphorus is needed for the backbone of DNA and for ATP manufacturing.

Role of decomposers in nutrient cycling

Decomposers recycle the carbon accumulated in durable organic material that does not immediately proceed to the carbon cycle. Ammonification is the decomposition of organic nitrogen back to ammonia. This process in the nitrogen cycle is carried out by aerobic and anaerobic bacterial and fungal decomposers. Decomposers add phosphorous back to the soil by decomposing the excretion of animals.

0030 Understand human ecology and the physical and societal effects of human activities on the environment

Human population dynamics

The human population has been growing exponentially for centuries. People are living longer and healthier lives than ever before. Better health care and nutrition practices have helped in the survival of the population.

Human activity affects parts of the nutrient cycles by removing nutrients from one part of the biosphere and adding them to another. This results in nutrient depletion in one area and nutrient excess in another. This affects water systems, crops, wildlife, and humans.

Human use of natural resources

Humans have a tremendous impact on the world's natural resources. Human use affects the world's natural water supplies. Waterways are major sources for recreation and freight transportation. Oil and wastes from boats and cargo ships pollute the aquatic environment. This contamination affects aquatic plant and animal life.

Deforestation for urban development has resulted in the extinction or relocation of several species of plants and animals. Animals are forced to leave their forest homes. The number of plant and animal species that have become extinct due to deforestation is unknown. Scientists have only identified a fraction of the species on Earth.

Sample Test

Directions: Read each item and select the best response.

1. A student designed a science project testing the effects of light and water on plant growth. You would recommend that she...(Skill 0001) (Average Rigor)

   A. manipulate the temperature as well.

   B. also alter the pH of the water as another variable.

   C. omit either water or light as a variable.

   D. also alter the light concentration as another variable.

2. Two hundred plants were grown. Fifty plants died. What percentage of the plants survived? (Skill 0001) (Easy Rigor)

   A. 40%

   B. 25%

   C. 75%

   D. 50%

3. Three plants were grown. The following data was taken. Determine the mean growth. Plant 1: 10cm Plant 2: 20cm Plant 3: 15cm (Skill 0001) (Easy Rigor)

   A. 5 cm

   B. 45 cm

   C. 12 cm

   D. 15 cm

4. The reading of a meniscus in a graduated cylinder is done at the... (Skill 0001) (Average Rigor)

   A. top of the meniscus.

   B. middle of the meniscus.

   C. bottom of the meniscus.

   D. closest whole number.

5. In an experiment measuring the growth of bacteria at different temperatures, identify the independent variable. (Skill 0001) (Average Rigor)

   A. growth of number of colonies

   B. temperature

   C. type of bacteria used

   D. light intensity

6. Identify the control in the following experiment. A student grew four plants under the following conditions and was measuring photosynthetic rate by measuring mass. 2 plants in 50% light and 2 plants in 100% light. (Skill 0002) (Rigorous)

A. plants grown with no added nutrients

B. plants grown in the dark

C plants in 100% light

D. plants in 50% light

7. A scientific theory... (Skill 0002) (Easy Rigor)

A. proves scientific accuracy.

B. is never rejected.

C. results in a medical breakthrough.

D. may be altered at a later time.

8. Which is the correct order of methodology? 1) testing revised explanation, 2) setting up a controlled experiment to test an explanation, 3) drawing a conclusion, 4) suggesting an explanation for observations, and 5) comparing observed results to hypothesized results (Skill 0002) (Rigorous)

A. 4, 2, 3, 1, 5

B. 3, 1, 4, 2, 5

C. 4, 2, 5, 1, 3

D. 2, 5, 4, 1, 3

9. Given a choice, which is the most desirable method of heating a substance in the lab? (Skill 0003) (Easy Rigor)

A. alcohol burner

B. gas burner

C. Bunsen burner

D. hot plate

10. Which is not a correct statement regarding the use of a light microscope? (Skill 0003) (Average Rigor)

A. carry the microscope with two hands

B. store on the low power objective

C. clean all lenses with lens paper

D. Focus first on high power

11. **Spectrophotometry utilizes the principle of... (Skill 0003) (Rigorous)**

    A.   light transmission.

    B.   molecular weight.

    C.   solubility of the substance.

    D.   electrical charges.

12. **Biological waste should be disposed of... (Skill 0003) (Easy Rigor)**

    A. in the trash can.

    B. under a fume hood.

    C. in the broken glass box.

    D. in an autoclavable biohazard bag.

13. **Chemicals should be stored... (Skill 0003) (Easy Rigor)**

    A. in a cool dark room.

    B. in a dark room.

    C. according to their reactivity with other substances.

    D. in a double locked room.

14. **Chromatography is most often associated with the separation of... (Skill 0003) (Average Rigor)**

    A. nutritional elements.

    B. DNA.

    C. proteins.

    D. plant pigments.

15. **Given the choice of lab activities, which would you omit? (Skill 0003) (Average Rigor)**

    A. a genetics experiment tracking the fur color of mice

    B. dissecting a preserved fetal pig

    C. a lab relating temperature to respiration rate using live goldfish

    D. pithing a frog to see the action of circulation

16. **Who should be notified in the case of a serious chemical spill? (Skill 0003) (Average Rigor)**

    I.   the custodian
    II. the fire department
    III. the chemistry teacher
    IV. the administration

    A. I

    B. II

    C. II and III

    D. II and IV

17. The "Right to Know" law states...
    (Skill 0003) (Average Rigor)

    A. the inventory of toxic
       chemicals checked against
       the "Substance List" be available.

    B. that students are to be informed
       of alternatives to dissection.

    C. that science teachers are to be
       informed of student allergies.

    D. that students are to be informed
       of infectious microorganisms
       used in lab.

18. In which situation would a
    science teacher be liable?
    (Skill 0003) (Average Rigor)

    A. a teacher leaves to receive an
       emergency phone call and a
       student slips and falls

    B. a student removes their goggles
       and gets dissection fluid in their
       eye

    C. a faulty gas line results in a fire

    D. a students cuts themselves with a
       scalpel

19. Which statement best defines
    negligence? (Skill 0003)
    (Rigorous)

    A. failure to give oral instructions for
       those with reading disabilities

    B. failure to exercise ordinary care

    C. inability to supervise a large
       group of students

    D. reasonable anticipation that an
       event may occur

20. Which item should always be
    used when using chemicals with
    noxious vapors? (Skill 0003)(Easy
    Rigor)

    A. eye protection

    B. face shield

    C. fume hood

    D. lab apron

21. A light microscope has an
    ocular of 10X and an
    objective of 40X. What is the
    total magnification?
    (Skill 0003) (Rigorous)

    A. 400X

    B. 30X

    C. 50X

    D. 4000X

22 Which scientists are credited with the discovery of the structure of DNA?
(Skill 0004) (Easy Rigor)

A. Hershey & Chase

B. Sutton & Morgan

C. Watson & Crick

D. Miller & Fox

23. A type of molecule not found in the membrane of an animal cell is...(Skill 0008) (Average Rigor)

A. phospholipid.

B. protein.

C. cellulose.

D. cholesterol.

24. Which process contributes to the large variety of living things in the world today?
(Skill 0008) (Average Rigor)

A. meiosis

B. asexual reproduction

C. mitosis

D. alternation of generations

25. Thermoacidophiles are...
(Skill 0008) (Rigorous)

A. prokaryotes.

B. eukaryotes.

C. bacteria.

D. archaea.

26. The Endosymbiotic theory states that...(Skill 0008) (Rigorous)

A. eukaryotic organelles arose from prokaryotes.

B. animals evolved in close relationships with one another.

C. the prokaryotes arose from eukaryotes.

D. life arose from inorganic compounds.

27. According to the fluid-mosaic model of the cell membrane, membranes are composed of...
(Skill 0008) (Rigorous)

A. phospholipid bilayers with proteins embedded in the layers.

B. one layer of phospholipids with cholesterol embedded in the layer.

C. two layers of protein with lipids embedded in the layers.

D. DNA and fluid proteins.

**28. Oxygen is given off in the...
(Skill 0008) (Average Rigor)**

A. light reactions of photosynthesis.

B. dark reactions of photosynthesis.

C. Krebs cycle.

D. reduction of NAD+ to NADH

**29. Potassium chloride is an
example of a(n)...
(Skill 0009) (Rigorous)**

A. non polar covalent bond.

B. polar covalent bond.

C. ionic bond.

D. hydrogen bond.

**30. Negatively charged particles
that circle the nucleus of an
atom are called...
(Skill 0009) (Average Rigor)**

A. neutrons.

B. neutrinos.

C. electrons.

D. protons.

**31. Which of the following is a
monomer? (Skill 0009) (Rigorous)**

A. RNA

B. glycogen

C. DNA

D. amino acid

**32. Sulfur oxides and nitrogen oxides
in the environment react with
water to cause... (Skill 0009)
(Rigorous)**

A. ammonia.

B. acidic precipitation.

C. sulfuric acid.

D. global warming.

**33. Which of the following are
properties of water?
(Skill 0009) (Average Rigor)
  I. High specific heat
  II. Strong ionic bonds
  III.Good solvent
  IV.High freezing point**

A. I, III, IV

B. II and III

C. I and II

D. II, III, IV

**34. Which does not affect enzyme
rate? (Skill 0010) (Average Rigor)**

A. increase of temperature

B. amount of substrate

C. pH

D. size of the cell

35. The loss of an electron is
_____ and the gain of an
electron is _____.
(Skill 0010) (Average Rigor)

A. oxidation, reduction

B. reduction, oxidation

C. glycolysis, photosynthesis

D. photosynthesis, glycolysis

36. The product of anaerobic
respiration in animals is...
(Skill 0010) (Rigorous)

A. carbon dioxide.

B. lactic acid.

C. pyruvate.

D. ethyl alcohol.

37. Carbon dioxide is fixed in the
form of glucose in...
(Skill 0010) (Average Rigor)

A. the Krebs cycle.

B. the light reactions.

C. the dark reactions (Calvin cycle).

D. glycolysis.

38. Which type of cell would contain
the most mitochondria?
(Skill 0010) (Rigorous)

A. muscle cell

B. nerve cell

C. epithelium

D. blood cell

39. During the Krebs cycle, 8 carrier
molecules are formed. What are
they?(Skill 0010) (Rigorous)

A. 3 NADH, 3 FADH, 2 ATP

B. 6 NADH and 2 ATP

C. 4 $FADH_2$ and 4 ATP

D. 6 NADH and 2 $FADH_2$

40. What is necessary for diffusion
to occur? (Skill 0010) (Average
Rigor)

A. carrier proteins

B. energy

C. a concentration gradient

D. a membrane

41. Which is an example of the use of energy to move a substance through a membrane from areas of low concentration to areas of high concentration?
(Skill 0010) (Average Rigor)

  A. osmosis

  B. active transport

  C. exocytosis

  D. phagocytosis

42. A plant cell is placed in salt water. The resulting movement of water out of the cell is called...
(Skill 0010) (Rigorous)

  A. facilitated diffusion.

  B. diffusion.

  C. transpiration.

  D. osmosis.

43. In the electron transport chain, all the following are true except...
(Skill 0010) (Average Rigor)

  A. it occurs in the mitochondrion.

  B. it does not make ATP directly.

  C. the net gain of energy is 30 ATP.

  D. most molecules in the electron transport chain are proteins.

44. As the amount of waste production increases in a cell, the rate of excretion...
(Skill 0010) (Average Rigor)

  A. slowly decreases.

  B. remains the same.

  C. increases.

  D. stops due to cell death.

45. All the following statements regarding both a mitochondria and a chloroplast are correct except...(Skill 0010) (Average Rigor)

  A. they both produce energy over a gradient.

  B. they both have DNA and are capable of reproduction.

  C. they both transform light energy to chemical energy.

  D. they both make ATP.

46. The shape of a cell depends on its...(Skill 0010) (Average Rigor)

  A. function.

  B. structure.

  C. age.

  D. size.

47. The most ATP is generated through... (Skill 0010) (Rigorous)

   A. fermentation.

   B. glycolysis.

   C. chemiosmosis.

   D. the Krebs cycle.

48. Oxygen created in photosynthesis comes from the breakdown of... (Skill 0010) (Easy Rigor)

   A. carbon dioxide.

   B. water.

   C. glucose.

   D. carbon monoxide.

49. Which photosystem makes ATP? (Skill 0010)(Rigorous)

   A. photosystem I

   B. photosystem II

   C. photosystem III

   D. photosystem IV

50. This stage of mitosis includes cytokinesis or division of the cytoplasm and its organelles. (Skill 0011) (Average Rigor)

   A. anaphase

   B. interphase

   C. prophase

   D. telophase

51. Replication of chromosomes occurs during which phase of the cell cycle? (Skill 0011) (Average Rigor)

   A. prophase

   B. interphase

   C. metaphase

   D. anaphase

52. Which statement regarding mitosis is correct?(Skill 0011) (Rigorous)

   A. diploid cells produce haploid cells for sexual reproduction

   B. sperm and egg cells are produced

   C. diploid cells produce diploid cells for growth and repair

   D. it allows for greater genetic diversity

53. In a plant cell, telophase is described as...(Skill 0011) (Average Rigor)

   A. the time of chromosome doubling.

   B. cell plate formation.

   C. the time when crossing over occurs.

   D. cleavage furrow formation.

54. Which of the following is not a type of fiber that makes up the cytoskeleton? (Skill 0011) (Rigorous)

   A. vacuoles

   B. microfilaments

   C. microtubules

   D. intermediate filaments

55. Identify this stage of mitosis. (Skill 0011) (Rigorous)

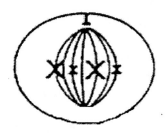

   A. anaphase

   B. metaphase

   C. telophase

   D. prophase

56. The area of a DNA nucleotide that varies is the... (Skill 0011) (Rigorous)

   A. deoxyribose.

   B. phosphate group.

   C. nitrogenous base.

   D. sugar.

57. Identify this stage of mitosis. Skill 0011) (Rigorous)

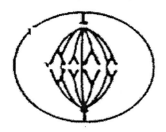

   A. anaphase

   B. metaphase

   C. prophase

   D. telophase

58. Cancer cells divide extensively and invade other tissues. This continuous cell division is due to...(Skill 0011) (Rigorous)

   A. density dependent inhibition.

   B. density independent inhibition.

   C. chromosome replication.

   D. growth factors.

59. Identify this stage of mitosis.
    (Skill 0011) (Rigorous)

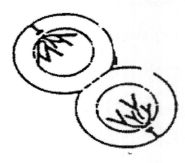

A. prophase

B. telophase

C. anaphase

D. metaphase

60. Which phylum accounts for 85%
    of all animal species?
    (Skill 0012) (Easy Rigor)

A. Nematoda

B. Chordata

C. Arthropoda

D. Cnidaria

61. The wing of a bird, human arm,
    and whale flipper have the same
    bone structure. These are
    called...(Skill 0012) (Rigorous)

A. polymorphic structures.

B. homologous structures.

C. vestigial structures.

D. analogous structures.

62. The two major ways to
    determine taxonomic
    classification are...
    (Skill 0012) (Rigorous)

A. evolution and phylogeny.

B. reproductive success and
   evolution.

C. phylogeny and morphology.

D. size and color.

63. Man's scientific name is *Homo
    sapiens*. Choose the proper
    classification beginning with
    kingdom and ending with order.
    (Skill 0012) (Rigorous)

A. Animalia, Vertebrata, Mammalia,
   Primate, Hominidae

B. Animalia, Vertebrata, Chordata,
   Mammalia, Primate

C. Animalia, Chordata, Vertebrata,
   Mammalia, Primate

D. Chordata, Vertebrata, Primate,
   Homo, sapiens

64. The scientific name *Canis
    familiaris* refers to the animal's...
    (Skill 0012) (Average Rigor)

A. kingdom and phylum names

B. genus and species names

C. class and species names

D. order and family names

65. Members of the same species... (Skill 0012) (Easy Rigor)

A. look identical.

B. never change.

C. reproduce successfully within their group.

D. live in the same geographic location.

66. The first cells that evolved on earth were probably of which type?(Skill 0012) (Average Rigor)

A. autotrophs

B. eukaryotes

C. heterotrophs

D. prokaryotes

67. Identify the correct sequence of organization of living things. (Skill 0013) (Rigorous)

A. cell – organelle – organ – tissue – organ system – organism

B. cell – tissue – organ – organelle – organ system – organism

C. organelle – cell – tissue – organ – organ system – organism

D. organ system – tissue – organelle – cell – organism – organ

68. Which is not a defining characteristic of all living things? (Skill 0013) (Easy Rigor)

A. locomotion

B. cellular structure

C. metabolism

D. reproduction

69. Segments of DNA can be transferred from the DNA of one organism to another through the use of which of the following? (Skill 0013) (Average Rigor)

A. bacterial plasmids

B. viruses

C. chromosomes from frogs

D. plant DNA

70. Which protein structure consists of the coils and folds of polypeptide chains? (Skill 0013) (Rigorous)

A. secondary structure

B. quaternary structure

C. tertiary structure

D. primary structure

71. **Water movement to the top of a twenty foot tree is most likely due to which principle? (Skill 0013) (Average Rigor)**

    A. osmostic pressure

    B. xylem pressure

    C. capillarity

    D. transpiration

72. **Protists are classified into major groups according to... (Skill 0013) (Average Rigor)**

    A. their method of obtaining nutrition.

    B. reproduction.

    C. metabolism.

    D. their form and function.

73. **How are angiosperms different from other groups of plants? (Skill 0013) (Average Rigor)**

    A. presence of flowers and fruits

    B. production of spores for reproduction

    C. true roots and stems

    D. seed production

74. **Viruses are made of... (Skill 0013) (Rigorous)**

    A. a protein coat surrounding a nucleic acid.

    B. DNA, RNA, and a cell wall.

    C. a nucleic acid surrounding a protein coat.

    D. protein surrounded by DNA.

75. **Generations of plants alternate between... (Skill 0013) (Rigorous)**

    A. angiosperms and bryophytes.

    B. flowering and nonflowering stages.

    C. seed bearing and spore bearing plants.

    D. haploid and diploid stages.

76. **Double fertilization refers to which of the following? (Skill 0013) (Average Rigor)**

    A. two sperm fertilizing one egg

    B. fertilization of a plant by gametes from two separate plants

    C. two sperm enter the plant embryo sac; one sperm fertilizes the egg, the other forms the endosperm

    D. the production of non-identical twins through fertilization of two separate eggs

77. Characteristics of coelomates include: (Skill 0013) (Rigorous)
I. no true digestive system
II. two germ layers
III. true fluid filled cavity
IV. three germ layers

A. I

B. II and IV

C. IV

D. III and IV

78 In angiosperms, the food for the developing plant is found in which of the following structures?
(Skill 0013) (Average Rigor)

A. ovule

B. endosperm

C. male gametophyte

D. cotyledon

79. Which kingdom is comprised of organisms made of one cell with no nuclear membrane?
(Skill 0013) (Rigorous)

A. Monera

B. Protista

C. Fungi

D. Algae

80. A virus that can remain dormant until a certain environmental condition causes its rapid increase is said to be...
(Skill 0013) (Average Rigor)

A. lytic.

B. benign.

C. saprophytic.

D. lysogenic.

81. The process in which pollen grains are released from the anthers is called...(Skill 0013) (Easy Rigor)

A. pollination.

B. fertilization.

C. blooming.

D. dispersal.

82. Which of the following is not a characteristic of a monocot?
(Skill 0015) (Easy Rigor)

A. parallel veins in leaves

B. petals of flowers occur in multiples of 4 or 5

C. one seed leaf

D. vascular tissue scattered throughout the stem

83. **What controls gas exchange on the bottom of a plant leaf? (Skill 0015) (Average Rigor)**

   A. stomata

   B. epidermis

   C. collenchyma and schlerenchyma

   D. palisade mesophyll

84. **Spores are the reproduction mode for which of the following group of plants? (Skill 0015) (Average Rigor)**

   A. algae

   B. flowering plants

   C. conifers

   D. ferns

85. **Which is not considered to be a morphological type of bacteria? (Skill 0015) (Easy Rigor)**

   A. obligate

   B. coccus

   C. spirillum

   D. bacillus

86. **Antibiotics are effective in fighting bacterial infections due to their ability to... (Skill 0015) (Rigorous)**

   A. interfere with DNA replication in the bacteria.

   B. prevent the formation of new cell walls in the bacteria.

   C. disrupt the ribosome of the bacteria.

   D. All of the above.

87. **Bacteria commonly reproduce by a process called binary fission. Which of the following best defines this process? (Skill 0015) (Rigorous)**

   A. viral vectors carry DNA to new bacteria

   B. DNA from one bacterium enters another

   C. DNA doubles and the bacterial cell divides

   D. DNA from dead cells is absorbed into bacteria

88. **All of the following are members of the Kingdom Fungi except... (Skill 0015) (Easy Rigor)**

   A. mold.

   B. algae.

   C. mildew.

   D. mushrooms.

89. Which of the following is the correct order of the stages of plant development from egg to adult plant?(Skill 0015) (Rigorous)

    A. morphogenesis, growth, and cellular differentiation

    B. cell differentiation, growth, and morphogenesis

    C. growth, morphogenesis, and cellular differentiation

    D. growth, cellular differentiation, and morphogensis

90. In comparison to protist cells, moneran cells...(Skill 0015) (Average Rigor)
    I. are usually smaller.
    II. evolved later.
    III. are more complex.
    IV. contain more organelles.

    A. I

    B. I and II

    C. II and III

    D. I and IV

91. Which is the correct sequence of embryonic development in a frog? (Skill 0015) (Rigorous)

    A. cleavage – blastula – gastrula

    B. cleavage – gastrula – blastula

    C. blastula – cleavage – gastrula

    D. gastrula – blastula – cleavage

92. In the comparison of respiration to photosynthesis, which statement is true? (Skill 0015) (Rigorous)

    A. oxygen is a waste product in photosynthesis but not in respiration

    B. glucose is produced in respiration but not in photosynthesis

    C. carbon dioxide is formed in photosynthesis but not in respiration

    D. water is formed in respiration but not in photosynthesis

93. Using a gram staining technique, it is observed that E. coli stains pink. It is therefore... (Skill 0015) (Rigorous)

    A. gram positive.

    B. dead.

    C. gram negative.

    D. gram neutral.

94. After sea turtles are hatched on the beach, they start the journey to the ocean. This is due to... (Skill 0015) (Average Rigor)

    A. innate behavior.

    B. territoriality.

    C. the tide.

    D. learned behavior.

95. **All of the following are found in the dermis layer of skin except...** (Skill 0016) (Average Rigor)

    A. sweat glands.

    B. keratin.

    C. hair follicles.

    D. blood vessels.

96. **Movement is possible by the action of muscles pulling on...** (Skill 0016) (Easy Rigor)

    A. skin.

    B. bones.

    C. joints.

    D. ligaments.

97. **All of the following are functions of the skin except...** (Skill 0016) (Average Rigor)

    A. storage.

    B. protection.

    C. sensation.

    D. regulation of temperature.

98. **A bicyclist has a heart rate of 110 beats per minute and a stroke volume of 85 mL per beat. What is the cardiac output?** (Skill 0017) (Rigorous)

    A. 9.35 L/min

    B. 1.29 L/min

    C. 0.772 L/min

    D. 129 L/min

99. **A school age boy had the chicken pox as a baby. He will most likely not get this disease again because of...** (Skill 0017) (Average Rigor)

    A. passive immunity.

    B. vaccination.

    C. antibiotics.

    D. active immunity.

100. **If the niches of two species overlap, what usually results?** (Skill 0018)(Average Rigor)

    A. a symbiotic relationship

    B. cooperation

    C. competition

    D. a new species

101. A muscular adaptation to move food through the digestive system is called... (Skill 0019)(Easy Rigor)

A. peristalsis.

B. passive transport.

C. voluntary action.

D. bulk transport.

102. Food is carried through the digestive tract by a series of wave-like contractions. This process is called... (Skill 0019)(Average Rigor)

A. peristalsis.

B. chyme.

C. digestion.

D. absorption.

103. Fats are broken down by which substance? (Skill 0019)(Easy Rigor)

A. bile produced in the gall bladder

B. lipase produced in the gall bladder

C. glucagons produced in the liver

D. bile produced in the liver

104. The role of neurotransmitters in nerve action is... (Skill 0020)(Average Rigor)

A. to turn off the sodium pump.

B. to turn off the calcium pump.

C. to send impulses to neurons.

D. to send impulses to the body

105. Which is the correct statement regarding the human nervous system and the human endocrine system? (Skill 0020)(Average Rigor)

A. the nervous system maintains homeostasis whereas the endocrine system does not

B. endocrine glands produce neurotransmitters whereas nerves produce hormones

C. nerve signals travel on neurons whereas hormones travel through the blood

D. the nervous system involves chemical transmission whereas the endocrine system does not

106. Fertilization in humans usually occurs in the... (Skill 0021)(Average Rigor)

A. uterus.

B. ovary.

C. fallopian tubes.

D. vagina.

107. Hormones are essential to the regulation of reproduction. What organ is responsible for the release of hormones for sexual maturity?
(Skill 0021)(Rigorous)

A. pituitary gland

B. hypothalamus

C. pancreas

D. thyroid gland

108. The Law of Segregation defined by Mendel states that...
(Skill 0022)(Rigorous)

A. when sex cells form, the two alleles that determine a trait will end up on different gametes.

B. only one of two alleles is expressed in a heterozygous organism.

C. the allele expressed is the dominant allele.

D. alleles of one trait do not affect the inheritance of alleles on another chromosome.

109. When a white flower is crossed with a red flower, incomplete dominance can be seen by the production of which of the following?
(Skill 0022)(Average Rigor)

A. pink flowers

B. red flowers

C. white flowers

D. red and white flowers

110. Which process(es) result(s) in a haploid chromosome number?
(Skill 0022)(Easy Rigor)

A. both meiosis and mitosis

B. mitosis

C. meiosis

D. replication and division

111. Homozygous individuals...
(Skill 0022)(Easy Rigor)

A. have two different alleles.

B. are of the same species.

C. have the same features.

D. have a pair of identical alleles.

112. **Sutton observed that genes and chromosomes behaved the same. This led him to his theory which stated...**
    (Skill 0022)(Average Rigor)

    A. that meiosis causes chromosome separation.

    B. that linked genes are able to separate.

    C. that genes and chromosomes have the same function.

    D. that genes are found on chromosomes

113. **Crossing over, which increases genetic diversity, occurs during which stage(s)?**
    (Skill 0022)(Rigorous)

    A. telophase II in meiosis

    B. metaphase in mitosis

    C. interphase in both mitosis and meiosis

    D. prophase I in meiosis

114. **A child with type O blood has a father with type A blood and a mother with type B blood. The genotypes of the parents respectively would be which of the following?**
    (Skill 0022)(Rigorous)

    A. AA and BO

    B. AO and BO

    C. AA and BB

    D. AO and OO

115. **Any change that affects the sequence of bases in a gene is called a(n)...**
    (Skill 0022)(Average Rigor)

    A. deletion.

    B. polyploid.

    C. mutation.

    D. duplication.

116. **Genes function in specifying the structure of which molecules?**
    (Skill 0023)(Easy Rigor)

    A. carbohydrates

    B. lipids

    C. nucleic acids

    D. proteins

117. **Which of the following is not posttranscriptional processing? (Skill 0023)(Rigorous)**

   A. 5' capping

   B. intron splicing

   C. polypeptide splicing

   D. 3' polyadenylation

118. **DNA synthesis results in a strand that is synthesized continuously. This is the... (Skill 0023)(Rigorous)**

   A. lagging strand.

   B. leading strand.

   C. template strand.

   D. complementary strand.

119. **A DNA strand has the base sequence of TCAGTA. Its DNA complement would have the following sequence. (Skill 0023)(Rigorous)**

   A. ATGACT

   B. TCAGTA

   C. AGUCAU

   D. AGTCAT

120. **What is the correct order of steps in protein synthesis? (Skill 0023)(Average Rigor)**

   A. transcription, then replication

   B. transcription, then translation

   C. translation, then transcription

   D. replication, then translation

121. **This carries amino acids to the ribosome in protein synthesis. (Skill 0023)(Easy Rigor)**

   A. messenger RNA

   B. ribosomal RNA

   C. transfer RNA

   D. DNA

122. **A protein is sixty amino acids in length. This requires a coded DNA sequence of how many nucleotides? (Skill 0023)(Easy Rigor)**

   A. 20

   B. 30

   C. 120

   D. 180

123. **A DNA molecule has the**

sequence of ACT. What is
the anticodon of this molecule?
(Skill 0023)(Rigorous)

A. UGA

B. ACU

C. TGA

D. ACT

124. **In DNA, adenine bonds with
_____, while cytosine
bonds with _____.
(Skill 0023)(Rigorous)**

A. thymine/guanine

B. adenine/cytosine

C. cytosine/adenine

D. guanine/thymine

125. **The individual parts of cells are
best studied using a(n)...
(Skill 0003)(Average Rigor)**

A. ultracentrifuge.

B. phase-contrast microscope.

C. CAT scan.

D. electron microscope.

reaction...
(Skill 0024)(Rigorous)

A. is a group of polymerases.

B. is a technique for amplifying
DNA.

C. is a primer for DNA synthesis.

D. is synthesis of polymerase.

127. **Amniocentesis is...
(Skill 0024)(Easy Rigor)**

A. a non-invasive technique for
detecting genetic disorders.

B. a bacterial infection.

C. extraction of amniotic fluid.

D. removal of fetal tissue.

128. **A genetic engineering
advancement in the medical
field is...(Skill 0024)(Rigorous)**

A. gene therapy.

B. pesticides.

C. degradation of harmful
chemicals.

D. antibiotics.

126. **The polymerase chain**

129. **Electrophoresis separates DNA**

on the basis of...
(Skill 0024)(Average Rigor)

A. amount of current.

B. molecular size.

C. positive charge of the molecule.

D. solubility of the gel.

130. **Which of the following is not true regarding restriction enzymes?**
(Skill 0024)(Rigorous)

A. they do not aid in recombination procedures

B. they are used in genetic engineering

C. they are named after the bacteria in which they naturally occur

D. they identify and splice certain base sequences on DNA

131. **The *lac* operon**
(Skill 0024)(Rigorous)
I. contains the *lac Z, lac Y,* and *lac A* genes
II. converts glucose to lactose
III. contains a repressor
IV. is on when the repressor is activated

A. I

B. II

C. III and IV

D. I and III

132. **The term "phenotype" refers to**

which of the following?
(Skill 0025)(Average Rigor)

A. a condition which is heterozygous

B. the genetic makeup of an individual

C. a condition which is homozygous

D. how the genotype is expressed

133. **The ratio of brown-eyed to blue-eyed children from the mating of a blue-eyed male to a heterozygous brown-eyed female is expected to be which of the following?**
(Skill 0025)(Rigorous)

A. 2:1

B. 1:1

C. 1:0

D. 1:2

134. **The biological species concept applies to...**
(Skill 0025) (Rigorous)

A. asexual organisms.

B. extinct organisms.

C. sexual organisms.

D. fossil organisms.

135. **Reproductive isolation results**

in...(Skill 0025)(Easy Rigor)

A. extinction.

B. migration.

C. follilization.

D. speciation.

136. Which of the following factors will disrupt the Hardy-Weinberg law of equilibrium, leading to evolutionary change? (Skill 0026)(Average Rigor)

A. no mutations

B. non-random mating

C. no immigration or emigration

D. large population

137. Which aspect of science does not support evolution? (Skill 0026)(Rigorous)

A. comparative anatomy

B. organic chemistry

C. comparison of DNA among organisms

D. analogous structures

138. Evolution occurs in...

(Skill 0026)(Average Rigor)

A. individuals.

B. populations.

C. organ systems.

D. cells.

139. If a population is in Hardy-Weinberg equilibrium and the frequency of the recessive allele is .3, what percentage of the population is expected to be heterozygous? (Skill 0026)(Rigorous)

A. 9%

B. 49%

C. 42%

D. 21%

140. A clownfish is protected by the sea anemone's tentacles. In turn, the anemone receives uneaten food from the clownfish. This is an example of... (Skill 0027)(Average Rigor)

A. mutualism.

B. parasitism.

C. commensalism.

D. competition.

141. All of the following are

density-independent factors that affect a population except...
(Skill 0028)(Easy Rigor)

A. temperature.

B. rainfall.

C. predation.

D. soil nutrients.

142. **Primary succession occurs after...**
(Skill 0028)(Average Rigor)

A. nutrient enrichment.

B. a forest fire.

C. bare rock is exposed after a water table recedes.

D. a housing development is built.

143. **If DDT were present in an ecosystem, which of the following organisms would have the highest concentration in its system?**
(Skill 0028)(Rigorous)

A. grasshopper

B. eagle

C. frog

D. crabgrass

144. **Which biome is the most**

prevalent on Earth?
(Skill 0028)(Easy Rigor)

A. marine

B. desert

C. savanna

D. tundra

145. **Which of the following is not an abiotic factor?**
(Skill 0028)(Average Rigor)

A. temperature

B. rainfall

C. soil quality

D. bacteria

146. **High humidity and temperature stability are present in which of the following biomes?**
(Skill 0028)(Easy Rigor)

A. taiga

B. deciduous forest

C. desert

D. tropical rain forest

147. **Which trophic level has the**

highest ecological efficiency?
(Skill 0028)(Rigorous)

A. decomposers

B. producers

C. tertiary consumers

D. secondary consumers

148. All of the following gasses made up the primitive atmosphere except...
(Skill 0029)(Rigorous)

A. ammonia.

B. methane.

C. oxygen.

D. hydrogen.

149. Which term is not associated with the water cycle?

(Skill 0029)(Easy Rigor)

A. precipitation

B. transpiration

C. fixation

D. evaporation

150. In the growth of a population, the increase is exponential until carrying capacity is reached. This is represented by a(n)...
(Skill 0030)(Rigorous)

A. S curve.

B. J curve.

C. M curve.

D. L curve.

Answer Key

1. C	39. D	77. D	115. C
2. C	40. C	78. B	116. D
3. D	41. B	79. A	117. C
4. C	42. D	80. D	118. B
5. B	43. C	81. A	119. D
6. C	44. C	82. B	120. B
7. D	45. C	83. A	121. C
8. C	46. A	84. D	122. D
9. D	47. C	85. A	123. B
10. D	48. B	86. D	124. A
11. A	49. A	87. C	125. D
12. D	50. D	88. B	126. B
13. C	51. B	89. C	127. C
14. D	52. C	90. A	128. A
15. D	53. B	91. A	129. B
16. D	54. A	92. A	130. A
17. A	55. B	93. C	131. D
18. A	56. C	94. A	132. D
19. B	57. A	95. B	133. B
20. C	58. B	96. B	134. C
21. A	59. B	97. A	135. D
22. C	60. C	98. A	136. B
23. C	61. B	99. D	137. B
24. A	62. C	100. C	138. B
25. D	63. C	101. A	139. C
26. A	64. B	102. A	140. A
27. A	65. C	103. D	141. C
28. A	66. D	104. A	142. C
29. C	67. C	105. C	143. B
30. C	68. A	106. C	144. A
31. D	69. A	107. B	145. D
32. B	70. A	108. A	146. D
33. A	71. D	109. A	147. B
34. D	72. D	110. C	148. C
35. A	73. A	111. D	149. C
36. B	74. A	112. D	150. A
37. C	75. D	113. D	
38. A	76. C	114. B	

Rigor Table

Easy Rigor 20%	Average Rigor 40%	Average Rigor 40%
2, 3, 7, 9, 12, 13, 20, 22, 48, 60, 65, 68, 81, 82, 85 88, 96, 101, 103, 110, 111, 116, 121, 122, 127, 135, 141, 144, 146, 149	1, 4, 5, 10, 14, 15, 16,17, 18, 23, 24, 28, 30, 33, 34, 35, 37, 40, 41, 43, 44, 45, 46, 50, 51, 53, 64, 66, 69, 71, 72, 73, 76, 78, 80, 83, 84, 90, 94, 95, 97, 99, 100, 102, 104, 105, 106, 109, 112, 115, 120, 125, 129, 132, 136, 138, 140, 142, 145	6, 8, 11, 19, 21, 25, 26, 27, 29, 31, 32, 36, 38, 39, 42, 47, 49, 52, 54, 55, 56, 58, 59, 61, 62, 63, 67, 70, 74, 75, 77, 79, 86, 87, 89, 91, 92, 93, 98, 107, 108, 113, 114, 117, 118, 119, 123, 124, 126, 128, 130, 131, 133, 134, 137, 139, 143, 147, 148, 150

Rationales with Sample Questions

1. **A student designed a science project testing the effects of light and water on plant growth. You would recommend that she...(Skill 0001) (Average Rigor)**

    A. manipulate the temperature as well.
    B. also alter the pH of the water as another variable.
    C. omit either water or light as a variable.
    D. also alter the light concentration as another variable.

    C. In science, you should design experiments that only manipulate one variable at a time.

2. **Two hundred plants were grown. Fifty plants died. What percentage of the plants survived? (Skill 0001) (Easy Rigor)**

    A. 40%
    B. 25%
    C. 75%
    D. 50%

    C. This is a proportion. If 50 plants died, then 200 − 50 = 150 survived. The number of survivors is the numerator and the total number of plants grown is the denominator.

    $$\frac{150}{200} = 0.75$$ Multiply by 100 to get percent = 75% survive

3. **Three plants were grown. The following data was taken. Determine the mean growth.**
    Plant 1: 10cm Plant 2: 20cm Plant 3: 15cm (Skill 0001) (Easy Rigor)

    A. 5 cm
    B. 45 cm
    C. 12 cm
    D. 15 cm

    D. The mean growth is the average of the three growth heights.

    $$\frac{10 + 20 + 15}{3} = 15 \text{ cm average height}$$

4. **The reading of a meniscus in a graduated cylinder is done at the... (Skill 0001) (Average Rigor)**

A.   top of the meniscus.
B.   middle of the meniscus.
C.   bottom of the meniscus.
D.   closest whole number.

C. The graduated cylinder is the most common instrument used for measuring volume. It is important for the accuracy of the measurement to read the volume level of the liquid at the bottom of the meniscus. The meniscus is the curved surface of the liquid.

5. **In an experiment measuring the growth of bacteria at different temperatures, identify the independent variable. (Skill 0001) (Average Rigor)**

A.   growth of number of colonies
B.   temperature
C.   type of bacteria used
D.   light intensity

B. The experimenter controls the independent variable. Here, the temperature is controlled to determine its effect on the growth of bacteria (dependent variable).

6. **Identify the control in the following experiment. A student grew four plants under the following conditions and was measuring photosynthetic rate by measuring mass. 2 plants in 50% light and 2 plants in 100% light. (Skill 0002) (Rigorous)**

A.   plants grown with no added nutrients
B.   plants grown in the dark
C   plants in 100% light
D.   plants in 50% light

C. The 100% light plants are those to which the student will compare the 50% plants. 100% light is the normal condition or control.

7. A scientific theory... (Skill 0002) (Easy Rigor)

A.   proves scientific accuracy.
B.   is never rejected.
C.   results in a medical breakthrough.
D.   may be altered at a later time.

D. Scientific theory is usually accepted and verified information but can always be changed at any time.

8. Which is the correct order of methodology? 1) testing a revised explanation, 2) setting up a controlled experiment to test an explanation, 3) drawing a conclusion, 4) suggesting an explanation for observations, and 5) comparing observed results to hypothesized results (Skill 0002) (Rigorous)

A.   4, 2, 3, 1, 5
B.   3, 1, 4, 2, 5
C.   4, 2, 5, 1, 3
D.   2, 5, 4, 1, 3

C. The first step in scientific inquiry is posing a question. Next, you form a hypothesis to provide a plausible explanation. You then propose and perform an experiment to test the hypothesis. A comparison between the predicted and observed results is the next step. You next draw conclusions and determine whether the hypothesis is correct or incorrect. If incorrect, the next step is to form a new hypothesis and repeat the process.

9. Given a choice, which is the most desirable method of heating a substance in the lab? (Skill 0003) (Easy Rigor)

A.   alcohol burner
B.   gas burner
C.   Bunsen burner
D.   hot plate

D. A hotplate is the only heat source from the choices above that does not have an open flame. The use of a hot plate will reduce the risk of fire and injury to students.

10. Which is not a correct statement regarding the use of a light microscope? (Skill 0003) (Average Rigor)

A.   carry the microscope with two hands
B.   store on the low power objective
C.   clean all lenses with lens paper
D.   focus first on high power

D. Always begin focusing on low power. This allows for the observation of microorganisms in a larger field of view. Switch to high power once you have a microorganism in view on low power.

11. Spectrophotometry utilizes the principle of... (Skill 0003) (Rigorous)

A.   light transmission.
B.   molecular weight.
C.   solubility of the substance.
D.   electrical charges.

A. Spectrophotometry uses percent of light at different wavelengths absorbed and transmitted by a pigment solution.

12. Biological waste should be disposed of... (Skill 0003) (Easy Rigor)

A.   in the trash can.
B.   under a fume hood.
C.   in the broken glass box.
D.   in an autoclavable biohazard bag.

D. Biological material should never be stored near food or water used for human consumption. All biological material should be appropriately labeled. All blood and body fluids should be put in a well-contained container with a secure lid to prevent leaking. All biological waste should be disposed of in biological hazardous waste bags.

13. Chemicals should be stored... (Skill 0003) (Easy Rigor)

A.   in a cool dark room.
B.   in a dark room.
C.   according to their reactivity with other substances.
D.   in a double locked room.

C. All chemicals should be stored with other chemicals of similar reactivity. Failure to do so could result in an undesirable chemical reaction.

**14. Chromotography is most often associated with the separation of...
(Skill 0003) (Average Rigor)**

A. nutritional elements.
B. DNA.
C. proteins.
D. plant pigments.

D. Chromatography uses the principles of capillarity to separate substances such as plant pigments. Molecules of a larger size will move slower up the paper, whereas smaller molecules will move more quickly producing lines of pigment.

**15. Given the choice of lab activities, which would you omit? (Skill 0003)
(Average Rigor)**

A. a genetics experiment tracking the fur color of mice
B. dissecting a preserved fetal pig
C. a lab relating temperature to respiration rate using live goldfish
D. pithing a frog to see the action of circulation

D. Regulations prohibit the use of live vertebrate organisms in a way that may harm the animal. The observation of fur color in mice is not harmful to the animal and the use of live goldfish is acceptable because they are invertebrates. The dissection of a fetal pig is acceptable if it comes from a known origin.

**16. Who should be notified in the case of a serious chemical spill?
(Skill 0003) (Average Rigor)**

   I. the custodian
   II. the fire department
   III. the chemistry teacher
   IV. the administration

A. I
B. II
C. II and III
D. II and IV

D. For large spills, the school administration and the local fire department should be notified.

17. The "Right to Know" law states... (Skill 0003) (Average Rigor)

A.   the inventory of toxic chemicals checked against the "Substance List" be available.
B.   that students are to be informed of alternatives to dissection.
C.   that science teachers are to be informed of student allergies.
D.   that students are to be informed of infectious microorganisms used in lab.

A. The right to know law pertains to chemical substances in the lab. Employees should check the material safety data sheets and the substance list for potential hazards in the lab.

18. In which situation would a science teacher be liable? (Skill 0003) (Average Rigor)

A.   a teacher leaves to receive an emergency phone call and a student slips and falls
B.   a student removes their goggles and gets dissection fluid in their eye
C.   a faulty gas line results in a fire
D.   a students cuts themselves with a scalpel

A. A teacher has an obligation to be present in the lab at all times. If the teacher needs to leave, he/she must arrange for an appropriate substitute.

19. Which statement best defines negligence? (Skill 0003) (Rigorous)

A.   failure to give oral instructions for those with reading disabilities
B.   failure to exercise ordinary care
C.   inability to supervise a large group of students
D.   reasonable anticipation that an event may occur

B. Negligence is the failure to exercise ordinary or reasonable care.

20. Which item should always be used when using chemicals with noxious vapors? (Skill 0003)(Easy Rigor)

A.   eye protection
B.   face shield
C.   fume hood
D.   lab apron

C. Fume hoods are designed to protect the experimenter from chemical fumes. The three other choices do not prevent chemical fumes from entering the respiratory system.

21. **A light microscope has an ocular of 10X and an objective of 40X. What is the total magnification? (Skill 0003) (Rigorous)**

A. 400X
B. 30X
C. 50X
D. 4000X

A. To determine the total magnification of a microscope, multiply the ocular lens by the objective lens. Here, the ocular lens is 10X and the objective lens is 40X.

(10X) X (40X) = 400X total magnification

22. **Which scientists are credited with the discovery of the structure of DNA? (Skill 0004) (Easy Rigor)**

A. Hershey & Chase
B. Sutton & Morgan
C. Watson & Crick
D. Miller & Fox

C. In the 1950's, James Watson and Francis Crick identified the structure of a DNA molecule as that of a double helix.

23. **A type of molecule not found in the membrane of an animal cell is... (Skill 0008) (Average Rigor)**

A. phospholipid.
B. protein.
C. cellulose.
D. cholesterol.

C. Phospholipids, protein, and cholesterol are all found in animal cells. Cellulose, however, is only found in plant cells.

24. **Which process contributes to the large variety of living things in the world today? (Skill 0008) (Average Rigor)**

A. meiosis
B. asexual reproduction
C. mitosis
D. alternation of generations

A. During meiosis prophase I crossing over occurs. This exchange of genetic material between homologues increases diversity.

25. Thermoacidophiles are... (Skill 0008) (Rigorous)

A.   prokaryotes.
B.   eukaryotes.
C.   protists.
D.   archaea.

D. Thermoacidophiles, methanogens, and halobacteria are members of the archaea group. They are as different from prokaryotes as prokaryotes are from eukaryotes.

26. The Endosymbiotic theory states that... (Skill 0008) (Rigorous)

A.   eukaryotic organelles arose from prokaryotes.
B.   animals evolved in close relationships with one another.
C.   prokaryotes arose from eukaryotes.
D.   life arose from inorganic compounds.

A. The Endosymbiotic theory of the origin of eukaryotic organelles states that eukaryotic organelles arose from symbiotic groups of prokaryotic cells. According to this theory, smaller prokaryotes lived within larger prokaryotic cells, eventually evolving into chloroplasts and mitochondria.

27. According to the fluid-mosaic model of the cell membrane, membranes are composed of... (Skill 0008) (Rigorous)

A.   phospholipid bilayers with proteins embedded in the layers.
B.   one layer of phospholipids with cholesterol embedded in the layer.
C.   two layers of protein with lipids embedded the layers.
D.   DNA and fluid proteins.

A. Cell membranes are composed of two phospholipids with their hydrophobic tails sandwiched between their hydrophilic heads, creating a lipid bilayer. The membrane contains proteins embedded in the layer (integral proteins) and proteins on the surface (peripheral proteins).

28. Oxygen is given off in the... (Skill 0008) (Average Rigor)

A.   light reactions of photosynthesis.
B.   dark reactions of photosynthesis.
C.   Krebs cycle.
D.   reduction of NAD+ to NADH.

A. The conversion of solar energy to chemical energy occurs in the light reactions. Electrons are transferred by the absorption of light by chlorophyll and cause water to split, releasing oxygen as a waste product.

29. Potassium chloride is an example of a(n)... (Skill 0009) (Rigorous)

A.   non polar covalent bond.
B.   polar covalent bond.
C.   ionic bond.
D.   hydrogen bond.

C. Ionic bonds form when one electron is stripped away from its atom to join another atom. Ionic compounds are called salts and potassium chloride is a salt; therefore, potassium chloride is an example of an ionic bond.

30. Negatively charged particles that circle the nucleus of an atom are called... (Skill 0009) (Average Rigor)

A.   neutrons.
B.   neutrinos.
C.   electrons.
D.   protons.

C. Neutrons and protons make up the core of an atom. Neutrons have no charge and protons are positively charged. Electrons are the negatively charged particles that orbit the nucleus.

31. Which of the following is a monomer? (Skill 0009) (Rigorous)

A.   RNA
B.   glycogen
C.   DNA
D.   amino acid

D. A monomer is the simplest unit of structure for a particular macromolecule. Amino acids are the basic units that comprise a proteins. RNA and DNA are polymers consisting of nucleotides and glycogen is a polymer consisting of many molecules of glucose.

32. Sulfur oxides and nitrogen oxides in the environment react with water to cause... (Skill 0009) (Rigorous)

A.   ammonia.
B.   acidic precipitation.
C.   sulfuric acid.
D.   global warming.

B. Acidic precipitation is rain, snow, or fog with a pH less than 5.6. It is caused by sulfur oxides and nitrogen oxides that react with water in the air to form acids that fall down to Earth as precipitation.

33. **Which of the following are properties of water?**
    (Skill 0009) (Average Rigor)

    I. High specific heat
    II. Strong ionic bonds
    III. Good solvent
    IV. High freezing point

A.   I, III, IV
B.   II and III
C.   I and II
D.   II, III, IV

A. All are properties of water except strong ionic bonds. Water is held together by polar covalent bonds between hydrogen and oxygen.

34. **Which does not affect enzyme rate? (Skill 0010) (Average Rigor)**

A.   increase of temperature
B.   amount of substrate
C.   pH
D.   size of the cell

D. Temperature and pH can affect the rate of reaction of an enzyme. The amount of substrate affects the enzyme as well. The enzyme acts on the substrate. The more substrate, the slower the enzyme rate. Therefore, the only possible is D, the size of the cell, which has no effect on enzyme rate.

35. **The loss of an electron is _____ and the gain of an electron is _____. (Skill 0010) (Average Rigor)**

A.   oxidation, reduction
B.   reduction, oxidation
C.   glycolysis, photosynthesis
D.   photosynthesis, glycolysis

A. Oxidation-reduction reactions are also known as redox reactions. In respiration, energy is released by the transfer of electrons by this process. The oxidation phase of this reaction involves the loss of an electron and the reduction phase involves the gain of an electron.

36. **The product of anaerobic respiration in animals is...**
    (Skill 0010) (Rigorous)

A.   carbon dioxide.
B.   lactic acid.
C.   pyruvate.
D.   ethyl alcohol.

B. In anaerobic lactic acid fermentation, pyruvate is reduced by NADH to form lactic acid. This is the anaerobic process in animals. Alcoholic fermentation is the anaerobic process in yeast and some bacteria resulting in ethyl alcohol. Carbon dioxide and pyruvate are the products of aerobic respiration.

37. **Carbon dioxide is fixed in the form of glucose in... (Skill 0010)**
    (Average Rigor)

A.   the Krebs cycle.
B.   the light reactions.
C.   the dark reactions (Calvin cycle).
D.   glycolysis.

C. The ATP produced during the light reaction is needed to convert carbon dioxide to glucose in the Calvin cycle.

38. **Which type of cell would contain the most mitochondria? (Skill 0010)**
    (Rigorous)

A.   muscle cell
B.   nerve cell
C.   epithelium
D.   blood cell

A. Mitochondria are the site of cellular respiration where ATP is made. Muscle cells have the most mitochondria because they use a great deal of energy.

39. **During the Krebs cycle, 8 carrier molecules are formed. What are they?**
    (Skill 0010) (Rigorous)

A.   3 NADH, 3 FADH, 2 ATP
B.   6 NADH and 2 ATP
C.   4 $FADH_2$ and 4 ATP
D.   6 NADH and 2 $FADH_2$

D. For each molecule of CoA that enters the Kreb's cycle, you get 3 NADH and 1 $FADH_2$. There are 2 molecules of CoA so the total yield is 6 NADH and 2 $FADH_2$.

40. **What is necessary for diffusion to occur? (Skill 0010) (Average Rigor)**

A.   carrier proteins
B.   energy
C.   a concentration gradient
D.   a membrane

C. Diffusion is the ability of molecules to move from areas of high concentration to areas of low concentration (a concentration gradient).

41. **Which is an example of the use of energy to move a substance through a membrane from areas of low concentration to areas of high concentration? (Skill 0010) (Average Rigor)**

A.   osmosis
B.   active transport
C.   exocytosis
D.   phagocytosis

B. Active transport can move substances with or against the concentration gradient. This energy requiring process allows for molecules to move from areas of low concentration to areas of high concentration.

42. **A plant cell is placed in salt water. The resulting movement of water out of the cell is called... (Skill 0010) (Rigorous)**

A.   facilitated diffusion.
B.   diffusion.
C.   transpiration.
D.   osmosis.

D. Osmosis is simply the diffusion of water across a semi-permeable membrane. Water will diffuse out of the cell if there is less water on the outside of the cell.

43. **In the electron transport chain, all the following are true except... (Skill 0010) (Average Rigor)**

A.   it occurs in the mitochondrion.
B.   it does not make ATP directly.
C.   the net gain of energy is 30 ATP.
D.   most molecules in the electron transport chain are proteins.

C. The end result of the electron transport chain is 34 molecules of ATP.

44. As the amount of waste production increases in a cell, the rate of excretion... (Skill 0010) (Average Rigor)

A.   slowly decreases.
B.   remains the same.
C.   increases.
D.   stops due to cell death.

C. Homeostasis is the control of the differences between internal and external environments. Excretion is the homeostatic system that regulates the amount of waste in a cell. As the amount of waste increases, the rate of excretion will increase to maintain homeostasis.

45. All the following statements regarding both a mitochondria and a chloroplast are correct except... (Skill 0010) (Average Rigor)

A.   they both produce energy over a gradient.
B.   they both have DNA and are capable of reproduction.
C.   they both transform light energy to chemical energy.
D.   they both make ATP.

C. Cellular respiration does not transform light energy to chemical energy. Cellular respiration transfers electrons to release energy. Photosynthesis utilizes light energy to produce chemical energy.

46. The shape of a cell depends on its... (Skill 0010) (Average Rigor)

A.   function.
B.   structure.
C.   age.
D.   size.

A. In most living organisms, cellular structure is based on function.

47. The most ATP is generated through... (Skill 0010) (Rigorous)

A.   fermentation.
B.   glycolysis.
C.   chemiosmosis.
D.   the Krebs cycle.

C. The electron transport chain uses electrons to pump hydrogen ions across the mitochondrial membrane. This ion gradient is used to form ATP in a process called chemiosmosis. ATP is generated by the removal of hydrogen ions from NADH and $FADH_2$. This yields 34 ATP molecules.

**48. Oxygen created in photosynthesis comes from the breakdown of...
(Skill 0010) (Easy Rigor)**

A.   carbon dioxide.
B.   water.
C.   glucose.
D.   carbon monoxide.

B. In photosynthesis, water is split. The hydrogen atoms are pulled to carbon dioxide, which is taken in by the plant and ultimately reduced to make glucose. The oxygen from the water is given off as a waste product.

49. Which photosystem makes ATP? (Skill 0010)(Rigorous)

A.   photosystem I
B.   photosystem II
C.   photosystem III
D.   photosystem IV

A. Photosystem I is composed of a pair of chlorophyll *a* molecules. It makes ATP whose energy is needed to build glucose.

50. This stage of mitosis includes cytokinesis or division of the cytoplasm and its organelles. (Skill 0011) (Average Rigor)

A.   anaphase
B.   interphase
C.   prophase
D.   telophase

D. The last stage of the mitotic phase is telophase. Here, the two nuclei form, each with a full set of DNA. The cell is pinched into two cells and cytokinesis, or division of the cytoplasm and organelles, occurs.

51. Replication of chromosomes occurs during which phase of the cell cycle? (Skill 0011) (Average Rigor)

A.   prophase
B.   interphase
C.   metaphase
D.   anaphase

B. Interphase is the stage where the cell grows and copies the chromosomes in preparation for the mitotic phase.

52. **Which statement regarding mitosis is correct? (Skill 0011) (Rigorous)**

A.   diploid cells produce haploid cells for sexual reproduction
B.   sperm and egg cells are produced
C.   diploid cells produce diploid cells for growth and repair
D.   it allows for greater genetic diversity

C. The purpose of mitotic cell division is to provide growth and repair in body (somatic) cells. The cells begin as diploid and produce diploid cells.

53. **In a plant cell, telophase is described as... (Skill 0011) (Average Rigor)**

A.   the time of chromosome doubling.
B.   cell plate formation.
C.   the time when crossing over occurs.
D.   cleavage furrow formation.

B. During plant cell telophase, a cell plate is observed whereas a cleavage furrow is formed in animal cells.

54. **Which of the following is not a type of fiber that makes up the cytoskeleton? (Skill 0011) (Rigorous)**

A.   vacuoles
B.   microfilaments
C.   microtubules
D.   intermediate filaments

A. Vacuoles are mostly found in plants and hold stored food and pigments. The other three choices are fibers that make up the cytoskeleton found in both plant and animal cells.

55. Identify this stage of mitosis. (Skill 0011) (Rigorous)

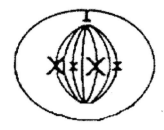

A.   anaphase
B.   metaphase
C.   telophase
D.   prophase

B. During metaphase, the centromeres are at opposite ends of the cell and the chromosomes align in the middle of the cell. Here, the chromosomes are aligned with one another.

56. The area of a DNA nucleotide that varies is the... (Skill 0011) (Rigorous)

A.   deoxyribose.
B.   phosphate group.
C.   nitrogenous base.
D.   sugar.

C. DNA is made of a 5-carbon sugar (deoxyribose), a phosphate group, and a nitrogenous base. There are four nitrogenous bases in DNA that allow for the four different nucleotides.

57. Identify this stage of mitosis. (Skill 0011) (Rigorous)

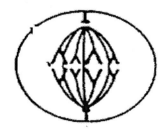

A.   anaphase
B.   metaphase
C.   prophase
D.   telophase

A. During anaphase, homologous chromosomes separate.

58. Cancer cells divide extensively and invade other tissues. This continuous cell division is due to... (Skill 0011) (Rigorous)

A.   density dependent inhibition.
B.   density independent inhibition.
C.   chromosome replication.
D.   growth factors.

B. Density dependent inhibition is when the cells crowd one another and consume all the nutrients, thereby halting cell division. Cancer cells, however, are density independent, meaning they can divide continuously as long as nutrients are present.

59. Identify this stage of mitosis. (Skill 0011) (Rigorous)

A.   prophase
B.   telophase
C.   anaphase
D.   metaphase

B. Telophase is the last stage of mitosis. Here, two nuclei become visible and the nuclear membrane reassembles.

60. Which phylum accounts for 85% of all animal species? (Skill 0012) (Easy Rigor)

A.   Nematoda
B.   Chordata
C.   Arthropoda
D.   Cnidaria

C. The arthropoda phylum consists of insects, crustaceans, and spiders. They are the largest group in the animal kingdom.

61. **The wing of a bird, human arm, and whale flipper have the same bone structure. These are called... (Skill 0012) (Rigorous)**

A.   polymorphic structures.
B.   homologous structures.
C.   vestigial structures.
D.   analogous structures.

B. Homologous structures have the same genetic basis (leading to similar appearances), but are used for different functions.

62. **The two major ways to determine taxonomic classification are... (Skill 0012) (Rigorous)**

A.   evolution and phylogeny.
B.   reproductive success and evolution.
C.   phylogeny and morphology.
D.   size and color.

C. Taxonomy is based on structure (morphology) and evolutionary relationships (phylogeny).

63. **Man's scientific name is Homo sapiens. Choose the proper classification beginning with kingdom and ending with order. (Skill 0012) (Rigorous**

A.   Animalia, Vertebrata, Mammalia, Primate, Hominidae
B.   Animalia, Vertebrata, Chordata, Mammalia, Primate
C.   Animalia, Chordata, Vertebrata, Mammalia, Primate
D.   Chordata, Vertebrata, Primate, Homo, sapiens

C. The order of classification for humans is as follows: Kingdom, Animalia; Phylum, Chordata; Subphylum, Vertebrata; Class, Mammalia; Order, Primate; Family, Hominadae; Genus, Homo; Species, sapiens.

64. **The scientific name *Canis familiaris* refers to the animal's... (Skill 0012)(Average Rigor**

A.   kingdom and phylum names.
B.   genus and species names.
C.   class and species names.
D.   order and family names.

B. Each species is scientifically known by a two-part name, or binomial. The first word in the name is the genus and the second word is its specific epithet (species name).

65. Members of the same species... (Skill 0012) (Easy Rigor)

A.   look identical.
B.   never change.
C.   reproduce successfully within their group.
D.   live in the same geographic location.

C. Species are defined by the ability to successfully reproduce with members of their own species.

66. The first cells that evolved on earth were probably of which type? (Skill 0012) (Average Rigor

A.   autotrophs
B.   eukaryotes
C.   heterotrophs
D.   prokaryotes

D. Prokaryotes date back to 3.5 billion years ago in the first fossil record. Their ability to adapt to the environment allows them to thrive in a wide variety of habitats.

67. Identify the correct sequence of organization of living things. (Skill 0013) (Rigorous)

A.   cell – organelle – organ system – tissue – organ – organism
B.   cell – tissue – organ – organ system – organelle – organism
C.   organelle – cell – tissue – organ – organ system – organism
D.   tissue – organelle – organ – cell – organism – organ system

C. An organism, such as a human, is comprised of several organ systems such as the circulatory and nervous systems. These organ systems consist of many organs including the heart and the brain. These organs are made of tissue such as cardiac muscle. Tissues are made up of cells, which contain organelles like the mitochondria and the Golgi apparatus.

68. Which is not a defining characteristic of all living things? (Skill 0013)(Easy Rigor)

A.   locomotion
B.   cellular structure
C.   metabolism
D.   reproduction

A. Locomotion is not a characteristic of all living things. For example, plants do not move from place to place.

69. Segments of DNA can be transferred from the genome of one organism to another through the use of which of the following? (Skill 0013) (Average Rigor)

A.   bacterial plasmids
B.   viruses
C.   chromosomes from frogs
D.   plant DNA

A. Plasmids can transfer themselves (and therefore their genetic information) by a process called conjugation. This requires cell-to-cell contact.

70. Which protein structure consists of the coils and folds of polypeptide chains? (Skill 0013) (Rigorous)

A.   secondary structure
B.   quaternary structure
C.   tertiary structure
D.   primary structure

A. Primary structure is the protein's unique sequence of amino acids. Secondary structure is the coils and folds of polypeptide chains. The coils and folds are the result of hydrogen bonds along the polypeptide backbone. Tertiary structure is formed by bonding between the side chains of the amino acids. Quaternary structure is the overall structure of the protein from the aggregation of two or more polypeptide chains.

71. Water movement to the top of a twenty foot tree is most likely due to which principle? (Skill 0013) (Average Rigor)

A.   osmotic pressure
B.   xylem pressure
C.   capillarity
D.   transpiration

D. Xylem is the tissue that transports water upward. Transpiration is the force that pulls the water upwards.

72. **Protists are classified into major groups according to... (Skill 0013)**
    (Average Rigor)

A.   their method of obtaining nutrition.
B.   reproduction.
C.   metabolism.
D.   their form and function.

D. The chaotic status of names and concepts of the higher classification of the protists reflects their great diversity in form, function, and life styles. The protists are often grouped as algae (plant-like), protozoa (animal-like), or fungus-like based on the similarity of their lifestyle and characteristics to these more defined groups.

73. **How are angiosperms different from other groups of plants?**
    (Skill 0013) (Average Rigor)

A.   presence of flowers and fruits
B.   production of spores for reproduction
C.   true roots and stems
D.   seed production

A. Angiosperms do not have spores for reproduction. They do have true roots and stems, as do all vascular plants. They do have seed production, as do the gymnosperms. The presence of flowers and fruits is the difference between angiosperms and other plants.

74. **Viruses are made of... (Skill 0013) (Rigorous)**

A.   a protein coat surrounding a nucleic acid.
B.   DNA, RNA, and a cell wall.
C.   a nucleic acid surrounding a protein coat.
D.   protein surrounded by DNA.

A. Viruses are composed of a protein coat and a nucleic acid, either RNA or DNA.

75. Generations of plants alternate between... (Skill 0013) (Rigorous)

A. angiosperms and bryophytes.
B. flowering and nonflowering stages.
C. seed bearing and spore bearing plants.
D. haploid and diploid stages.

D. Reproduction of plants is accomplished through alteration of generations. Simply stated, a haploid stage in the plant's life history alternates with a diploid stage.

76. Double fertilization refers to which of the following? (Skill 0013) (Average Rigor)

A. two sperm fertilizing one egg
B. fertilization of a plant by gametes from two separate plants
C. two sperm enter the plant embryo sac; one sperm fertilizes the egg, the other forms the endosperm
D. the production of non-identical twins through fertilization of two separate eggs

C. In angiosperms, double fertilization is when two sperm fertilize one ovum. One sperm produces the new plant and the other forms the food supply for the developing plant (endosperm).

77. Characteristics of coelomates include: (Skill 0013) (Rigorous)

I. no true digestive system
II. two germ layers
III. true fluid filled cavity
IV. three germ layers

A. I
B. II and IV
C. IV
D. III and IV

D. Coelomates are triplobastic animals (3 germ layers). They have a true fluid filled body cavity called a coelom.

78. **In angiosperms, the food for the developing plant is found in which of the following structures? (Skill 0013) (Average Rigor)**

A.   ovule
B.   endosperm
C.   male gametophyte
D.   cotyledon

B. The endosperm is a product of double fertilization. It is the food supply for the developing plant.

79. **Which kingdom is comprised of organisms made of one cell with no nuclear membrane? (Skill 0013) (Rigorous)**

A.   Monera
B.   Protista
C.   Fungi
D.   Algae

A. Monera is the only kingdom that is made up of unicellular organisms with no nucleus. Algae is a protist because it is made up of one type of tissue and it has a nucleus.

80. **A virus that can remain dormant until a certain environmental condition causes its rapid increase is said to be... (Skill 0013) (Average Rigor**

A.   lytic.
B.   benign.
C.   saprophytic.
D.   lysogenic.

D. A lysogenic virus remains dormant until something stimulates it to break out of the host cell.

81. **The process in which pollen grains are released from the anthers is called... (Skill 0013) (Easy Rigor)**

A.   pollination.
B.   fertilization.
C.   blooming.
D.   dispersal.

A. Pollen grains are released from the anthers during pollination and carried by animals and the wind to land on the carpels.

82. **Which of the following is not a characteristic of a monocot? (Skill 0015) (Easy Rigor)**

A. parallel veins in leaves
B. petals of flowers occur in multiples of 4 or 5
C. one seed leaf
D. vascular tissue scattered throughout the stem

B. Monocots have one cotelydon, parallel veins in their leaves, and their flower petals are in multiples of threes. Dicots have flower petals in multiples of fours and fives.

83. **What controls gas exchange on the bottom of a plant leaf? (Skill 0015) (Average Rigor)**

A. stomata
B. epidermis
C. collenchyma and schlerenchyma
D. palisade mesophyll

A. Stomata are openings on the underside of leaves that allow oxygen to move in or out of the plant and for carbon dioxide to move in.

84. **Spores are the reproduction mode for which of the following group of plants? (Skill 0015) (Average Rigor)**

A. algae
B. flowering plants
C. conifers
D. ferns

D. Ferns are non-seeded vascular plants. All plants in this group have spores and require water for reproduction.

85. **Which is not considered to be a morphological type of bacteria? (Skill 0015) (Easy Rigor)**

A. obligate
B. coccus
C. spirillum
D. bacillus

A. Morphology is the shape of an organism. Obligate is term used when describing dependence on something. Coccus is a round bacterium, spirillum is a spiral-shaped bacterium, and bacillus is a rod-shaped bacterium.

86. Antibiotics are effective in fighting bacterial infections due to their ability to... (Skill 0015) (Rigorous)

A.   interfere with DNA replication in the bacteria.
B.   prevent the formation of new cell walls in the bacteria.
C.   disrupt the ribosome of the bacteria.
D.   All of the above.

D. Different classes of antibiotics can destroy the bacterial cell wall, interfere with bacterial DNA replication, and disrupt the bacterial ribosome without affecting the host cells.

87. Bacteria commonly reproduce by a process called binary fission. Which of the following best defines this process? (Skill 0015) (Rigorous)

A.   viral vectors carry DNA to new bacteria
B.   DNA from one bacterium enters another
C.   DNA doubles and the bacterial cell divides
D.   DNA from dead cells is absorbed into bacteria

C. Binary fission is the asexual process in which the bacteria divide in half after the DNA doubles. This results in an exact clone of the parent cell.

88. All of the following are examples of a member of Kingdom Fungi except... (Skill 0015) (Easy Rigor)

A.   mold.
B.   algae.
C.   mildew.
D.   mushrooms.

B. Mold, mildew, and mushrooms are all fungi. Brown algae and golden algae are members of the kingdom protista and green algae are members of the plant kingdom.

89. Which of the following is the correct order of the stages of plant development from egg to adult plant? (Skill 0015)(Rigorous)

A.   morphogenesis, growth, and cellular differentiation
B.   cell differentiation, growth, and morphogenesis
C.   growth, morphogenesis, and cellular differentiation
D.   growth, cellular differentiation, and morphogensis

C. The development of the egg to form a plant occurs in three stages: growth; morphogenesis, the development of form; and cellular differentiation, the acquisition of a cell's specific structure and function.

90. In comparison to protist cells, moneran cells...
    (Skill 0015) (Average Rigor)

   I. are usually smaller
   II. evolved later
   III. are more complex
   IV. contain more organelles

A.   I
B.   I and II
C.   II and III
D.   I and IV

A. Moneran cells are almost always smaller than protists. Moneran cells are prokaryotic; therefore, they are less complex and have no organelles. Prokaryotes were the first cells on Earth and therefore evolved before the eukaryotic protists.

91. Which is the correct sequence of embryonic development in a frog? (Skill 0015) (Rigorous)

A.   cleavage – blastula – gastrula
B.   cleavage – gastrula – blastula
C.   blastula – cleavage – gastrula
D.   gastrula – blastula – cleavage

A.   Animals go through several stages of development after fertilization of the egg cell. The first step is cleavage, which continues until the egg becomes a blastula. The blastula is a hollow ball of undifferentiated cells. Gastrulation is the next step. This is the time of tissue differentiation into the separate germ layers: the endoderm, mesoderm, and ectoderm.

92. In the comparison of respiration to photosynthesis, which statement is true? (Skill 0015) (Rigorous)

A.   oxygen is a waste product in photosynthesis but not in respiration
B.   glucose is produced in respiration but not in photosynthesis
C.   carbon dioxide is formed in photosynthesis but not in respiration
D.   water is formed in respiration but not in photosynthesis

A.   In photosynthesis, water is split and the oxygen is given off as a waste product. In respiration, water and carbon dioxide are the waste products.

93. Using a gram staining technique, it is observed that *E. coli* stains pink. It is therefore... (Skill 0015) (Rigorous)

A.   gram positive.
B.   dead.
C.   gram negative.
D.   gram neutral.

C.   A Gram positive bacterium absorbs the stain and appears purple under a microscope because of its cell wall made of peptidoglycan. A Gram negative bacterium does not absorb the stain because of its more complex cell wall. These bacteria appear pink under a microscope.

94. **After sea turtles are hatched on the beach, they start the journey to the ocean. This is due to... (Skill 0015) (Average Rigor)**

A.   innate behavior.
B.   territoriality.
C.   the tide.
D.   learned behavior.

A. Innate behavior is inborn or instinctual. The baby sea turtles did not learn this behavior. They immediately knew to head towards the shore once they hatched.

95. **All of the following are found in the dermis layer of skin except... (Skill 0016) (Average Rigor)**

A.   sweat glands.
B.   keratin.
C.   hair follicles.
D.   blood vessels.

B. Keratin is a water proofing protein found in the epidermis.

96. **Movement is possible by the action of muscles pulling on... (Skill 0016) (Easy Rigor)**

A.   skin.
B.   bones.
C.   joints.
D.   ligaments.

B. The muscular system's function is for movement. Skeletal muscles attach to bones and are responsible for their movement.

97. **All of the following are functions of the skin except... (Skill 0016) (Average Rigor)**

A.   storage.
B.   protection.
C.   sensation.
D.   regulation of temperature.

A. Skin is a protective barrier against infection. It contains hair follicles that respond to sensation and it plays a role in thermoregulation.

98. **A bicyclist has a heart rate of 110 beats per minute and a stroke volume of 85 mL per beat. What is the cardiac output? (Skill 0017) (Rigorous)**

A. 9.35 L/min
B. 1.29 L/min
C. 0.772 L/min
D. 129 L/min

A. The cardiac output is the volume of blood per minute that is pumped into the systemic circuit. This is determined by multiplying the heart rate by the stroke volume. 110 * 85 = 9350 mL/min. Divide by 1000 to get units of liters. 9350/1000 = 9.35 L/min.

99. **A school age boy had the chicken pox as a baby. He will most likely not get this disease again because of... (Skill 0017) (Average Rigor)**

A. passive immunity.
B. vaccination.
C. antibiotics.
D. active immunity.

D. Active immunity develops after recovery from an infectious disease, such as the chicken pox, or after vaccination. Passive immunity may be passed from one individual to another (from mother to nursing child).

100. **If the niches of two species overlap, what usually results? (Skill 0018)(Average Rigor)**

A. a symbiotic relationship
B. cooperation
C. competition
D. a new species

C. Two species that occupy the same habitat or eat the same food are said to be in competition with each other.

101. A muscular adaptation to move food through the digestive system is called... (Skill 0019)(Easy Rigor)

A.   peristalsis.
B.   passive transport.
C.   voluntary action.
D.   bulk transport.

A. Peristalsis is a process of wave-like contractions. This process allows food to be carried down the pharynx and though the digestive tract.

102. Food is carried through the digestive tract by a series of wave-like contractions. This process is called... (Skill 0019)(Average Rigor)

A.   peristalsis.
B.   chyme.
C.   digestion.
D.   absorption.

A. Peristalsis is the process of wave-like contractions that moves food through the digestive tract.

103. Fats are broken down by which substance? (Skill 0019)(Easy Rigor)

A.   bile produced in the gall bladder
B.   lipase produced in the gall bladder
C.   glucagons produced in the liver
D.   bile produced in the liver

D. The liver produces bile, which breaks down and emulsifies fatty acids

104. The role of neurotransmitters in nerve action is... (Skill 0020)(Average Rigor)

A.   to turn off the sodium pump.
B.   to turn off the calcium pump.
C.   to send impulses to neurons.
D.   to send impulses to the body.

A. The neurotransmitters turn off the sodium pump, which results in depolarization of the membrane.

105. Which is the correct statement regarding the human nervous system and the human endocrine system? (Skill 0020)(Average Rigor)

A. the nervous system maintains homeostasis whereas the endocrine system does not
B. endocrine glands produce neurotransmitters whereas nerves produce hormones
C. nerve signals travel on neurons whereas hormones travel through the blood
D. the nervous system involves chemical transmission whereas the endocrine system does not

C. In the human nervous system, neurons carry nerve signals to and from the cell body. Endocrine glands produce hormones that are carried through the body in the bloodstream.

106. Fertilization in humans usually occurs in the... (Skill 0021)(Average Rigor)

A. uterus.
B. ovary.
C. fallopian tubes.
D. vagina.

C. Fertilization of the egg by the sperm normally occurs in the fallopian tube. The fertilized egg is then implanted in the uterine lining for development.

107. Hormones are essential to the regulation of reproduction. What organ is responsible for the release of hormones for sexual maturity? (Skill 0021)(Rigorous)

A. pituitary gland
B. hypothalamus
C. pancreas
D. thyroid gland

B. The hypothalamus begins secreting hormones that help mature the reproductive system and stimulate development of the secondary sex characteristics.

**108. The Law of Segregation defined by Mendel states that...
(Skill 0022)(Rigorous)**

A.   when sex cells form, the two alleles that determine a trait will end up on different gametes.
B.   only one of two alleles is expressed in a heterozygous organism.
C.   the allele expressed is the dominant allele.
D.   alleles of one trait do not affect the inheritance of alleles on another chromosome.

A. The law of segregation states that the two alleles for each trait segregate into different gametes.

109. When a white flower is crossed with a red flower, incomplete dominance can be seen by the production of which of the following? (Skill 0022)(Average Rigor)

A.   pink flowers
B.   red flowers
C.   white flowers
D.   red and white flowers

A. Incomplete dominance is when the F_1 generation results in an appearance somewhere between the parents. Red flowers crossed with white flowers results in an F_1 generation with pink flowers.

110. Which process(es) result(s) in a haploid chromosome number? (Skill 0022)(Easy Rigor)

A.   both meiosis and mitosis
B.   mitosis
C.   meiosis
D.   replication and division

C. In meiosis, there are two consecutive cell divisions resulting in the reduction of the chromosome number by half (diploid to haploid).

111. Homozygous individuals... (Skill 0022)(Easy Rigor)

A.   have two different alleles.
B.   are of the same species.
C.   have the same features.
D.   have a pair of identical alleles.

D. Homozygous individuals have a pair of identical alleles and heterozygous individuals have two different alleles.

112. **Sutton observed that genes and chromosomes behaved the same. This led him to his theory which stated... (Skill 0022)(Average Rigor)**

A.   that meiosis causes chromosome separation.
B.   that linked genes are able to separate.
C.   that genes and chromosomes have the same function.
D.   that genes are found on chromosomes.

D. Sutton observed how mitosis and meiosis confirmed Mendel's theory on "factors". His Chromosome Theory states that genes are located on chromosomes.

113. **Crossing over, which increases genetic diversity, occurs during which stage(s)? (Skill 0022)(Rigorous)**

A.   telophase II in meiosis
B.   metaphase in mitosis
C.   interphase in both mitosis and meiosis
D.   prophase I in meiosis

D. During prophase I of meiosis, the replicated chromosomes condense and pair with their homologues in a process called synapsis. Crossing over, the exchange of genetic material between homologues to further increase diversity, occurs during prophase I.

114. **A child with type O blood has a father with type A blood and a mother with type B blood. The genotypes of the parents respectively would be which of the following? (Skill 0022)(Rigorous)**

A.   AA and BO
B.   AO and BO
C.   AA and BB
D.   AO and OO

B. Type O blood has 2 recessive O genes. A child receives one allele from each parent; therefore, each parent in this example must have an O allele. The father has type A blood with a genotype of AO and the mother has type B blood with a genotype of BO.

115. Any change that affects the sequence of bases in a gene is called a(n)... (Skill 0022)(Average Rigor)

A. deletion.
B. polyploid.
C. mutation.
D. duplication.

C. A mutation is an inheritable change in DNA. It may be an error in replication or a spontaneous rearrangement of one ore more segments of DNA. Deletion and duplication are types of mutations. Polyploidy is when and organism has more than two complete chromosome sets.

116. Genes function in specifying the structure of which molecules? (Skill 0023)(Easy Rigor)

A. carbohydrates
B. lipids
C. nucleic acids
D. proteins

D. Genes contain the sequence of nucleotides that code for amino acids. Amino acids are the building blocks of protein.

117. Which of the following is not posttranscriptional processing? (Skill 0023)(Rigorous)

A. 5' capping
B. intron splicing
C. polypeptide splicing
D. 3' polyadenylation

C. The removal of segments of polypeptides is a posttranslational process. The other three are methods of posttranscriptional processing.

118. DNA synthesis results in a strand that is synthesized continuously. This is the... (Skill 0023)(Rigorous)

A. lagging strand.
B. leading strand.
C. template strand.
D. complementary strand.

B. As DNA synthesis proceeds along the replication fork, one strand is replicated continuously (the leading strand) and the other strand is replicated discontinuously (the lagging strand).

119. A DNA strand has the base sequence of TCAGTA. Its DNA complement would have the following sequence.
(Skill 0023)(Rigorous)

A.   ATGACT
B.   TCAGTA
C.   AGUCAU
D.   AGTCAT

D. The complement strand to a single strand DNA molecule has a complementary sequence to the template strand. T pairs with A and C pairs with G. Therefore, the complement to TCAGTA is AGTCAT.

120. What is the correct order of steps in protein synthesis?
(Skill 0023)(Average Rigor)

A.   transcription, then replication
B.   transcription, then translation
C.   translation, then transcription
D.   replication, then translation

B. A DNA strand first undergoes transcription to get a complementary mRNA strand. Translation of the mRNA strand then occurs with tRNAs adding the appropriate amino acids, producing a protein as the final product.

121. This carries amino acids to the ribosome in protein synthesis.
(Skill 0023)(Easy Rigor)

A.   messenger RNA
B.   ribosomal RNA
C.   transfer RNA
D.   DNA

C. The tRNA molecule is specific for a particular amino acid. The tRNA has an anticodon sequence that is complementary to the codon. This specifies where the tRNA places the amino acid in protein synthesis.

122. A protein is sixty amino acids in length. This requires a coded DNA sequence of how many nucleotides? (Skill 0023)(Easy Rigor)

A.   20
B.   30
C.   120
D.   180

D. Each amino acid codon consists of 3 nucleotides. If there are 60 amino acids in a protein, then 60 x 30 = 180 nucleotides.

123. A DNA molecule has the sequence of ACT. What is the anticodon of this molecule? (Skill 0023)(Rigorous)

A.   UGA
B.   ACU
C.   TGA
D.   ACT

B. The DNA is first transcribed into mRNA. Here, the DNA has the sequence ACT; therefore, the complementary mRNA sequence is UGA (remember, in RNA, T is U). This mRNA sequence is the codon. The anticodon is the complement to the codon. The anticodon sequence will be ACU (remember, the anticodon is tRNA, so U replaces T).

124. In DNA, adenine bonds with ____, while cytosine bonds with ____. (Skill 0023)(Rigorous)

A.   thymine/guanine
B.   adenine/cytosine
C.   cytosine/adenine
D.   guanine/thymine

A. In DNA, adenine pairs with thymine and cytosine pairs with guanine because of their nitrogenous base structures.

**125. The individual parts of cells are best studied using a(n)...
(Skill 0003)(Average Rigor)**

A.   ultracentrifuge.
B.   phase-contrast microscope.
C.   CAT scan.
D.   electron microscope.

D. The scanning electron microscope uses a beam of electrons to pass through the specimen. The resolution is about 1000 times greater than that of a light microscope. This allows the scientist to view extremely small objects, such as the individual parts of a cell.

126. The polymerase chain reaction... (Skill 0024)(Rigorous)

A.   is a group of polymerases.
B.   is a technique for amplifying DNA.
C.   is a primer for DNA synthesis.
D.   is synthesis of polymerase.

B. PCR is a technique for large-scale amplification of DNA in a short period of time.

127. Amniocentesis is... (Skill 0024)(Easy Rigor)

A.   a non-invasive technique for detecting genetic disorders.
B.   a bacterial infection.
C.   extraction of amniotic fluid.
D.   removal of fetal tissue.

C. Amniocentesis is a procedure in which a needle is inserted into the uterus to extract some of the amniotic fluid surrounding the fetus. Some genetic disorders can be detected by chemicals in the fluid.

128. A genetic engineering advancement in the medical field is...
(Skill 0024) (Rigorous)

A.   gene therapy.
B.   pesticides.
C.   degradation of harmful chemicals.
D.   antibiotics.

A. Gene therapy is the introduction of a normal allele to the somatic cells to replace a defective allele. The medical field has had success using gene therapy to treat patients with a single enzyme deficiency disease. Gene therapy has allowed doctors and scientists to introduce a normal allele that provides the missing enzyme.

129. Electrophoresis separates DNA on the basis of...
(Skill 0024)(Average Rigor)

A.   amount of current.
B.   molecular size.
C.   positive charge of the molecule.
D.   solubility of the gel.

B. Electrophoresis uses electrical charges of molecules to separate them according to their size.

130. Which of the following is not true regarding restriction enzymes?
(Skill 0024)(Rigorous)

A.   they do not aid in recombination procedures
B.   they are used in genetic engineering
C.   they are named after the bacteria in which they naturally occur
D.   they identify and splice certain base sequences on DNA

A. A restriction enzyme is a bacterial enzyme that cuts foreign DNA at specific locations. The splicing of restriction fragments into a plasmid results in a recombinant plasmid.

131. The *lac* operon (Skill 0024)(Rigorous)
   I. contains the *lac Z, lac Y,* and *lac A*
      genes
   II. converts glucose to lactose
   III. contains a repressor
   IV. is on when the repressor is
      activated

A.   I
B.   II
C.   III and IV
D.   I and III

D. The *lac* operon contains the genes that code for the enzymes used to convert lactose into fuel. It contains three genes: *lac A, lac Z,* and *lac Y*. It also contains a promoter and repressor. When the repressor is activated, the operon is off.

132. The term "phenotype" refers to which of the following?
   (Skill 0025)(Average Rigor)

A.   a condition which is heterozygous
B.   the genetic makeup of an individual
C.   a condition which is homozygous
D.   how the genotype is expressed

D. Phenotype is the physical appearance of an organism due to its genetic make-up (genotype).

133. The ratio of brown-eyed to blue-eyed children from the mating of a blue-eyed male to a heterozygous brown-eyed female is expected to be which of the following? (Skill 0025)(Rigorous)

A.   2:1
B.   1:1
C.   1:0
D.   1:2

B. Use a Punnet square to determine the ratio.

	b	b
B	Bb	Bb
b	bb	bb

B = brown eyes, b = blue eyes

Female genotype is on the side and the male genotype is across the top.

TEACHER CERTIFICATION STUDY GUIDE

The female is heterozygous and her phenotype is brown eyes. This means the dominant allele is for brown eyes. The male expresses the homozygous recessive allele for blue eyes. Their children are expected to have a ratio of brown eyes to blue eyes of 2:2 or 1:1.

134. The biological species concept applies to... (Skill 0025)(Rigorous)

A.   asexual organisms.
B.   extinct organisms.
C.   sexual organisms.
D.   fossil organisms.

C. The biological species concept states that a species is a reproductive community of populations that occupy a specific niche in nature. It focuses on reproductive isolation of populations as the primary criterion for recognition of species status. The biological species concept does not apply to organisms that are completely asexual in their reproduction, fossil organisms, or distinctive populations that hybridize.

135. Reproductive isolation results in... (Skill 0025)(Easy Rigor)

A.   extinction.
B.   migration.
C.   follilization.
D.   speciation.

D. Reproductive isolation is caused by any factor that impedes two species from producing viable, fertile hybrids. Reproductive isolation of populations is the primary criterion for recognition of species status.

136. Which of the following factors will disrupt the Hardy-Weinberg law of equilibrium, leading to evolutionary change? (Skill 0026)(Average Rigor)

A.   no mutations
B.   non-random mating
C.   no immigration or emigration
D.   large population

B. There are five requirements to keep the Hardy-Weinberg equilibrium stable: no mutation, no selection pressures, an isolated population, a large population, and random mating.

BIOLOGY   173

137. **Which aspect of science does not support evolution? (Skill 0026)(Rigorous)**

A.   comparative anatomy
B.   organic chemistry
C.   comparison of DNA among organisms
D.   analogous structures

B. Comparative anatomy is the comparison of characteristics of the anatomies of different species. This includes homologous structures and analogous structures. The comparison of DNA between species is the best known way to place species on the evolutionary tree. Organic chemistry has little to do with evolution.

138. **Evolution occurs in... (Skill 0026)(Average Rigor)**

A.   individuals.
B.   populations.
C.   organ systems.
D.   cells.

B. Evolution is a change in genotype over time. Gene frequencies shift and change from generation to generation. Populations evolve, not individuals.

139. **If a population is in Hardy-Weinberg equilibrium and the frequency of the recessive allele is 0.3, what percentage of the population is expected to be heterozygous? (Skill 0026)(Rigorous)**

A.   9%
B.   49%
C.   42%
D.   21%

C. 0.3 is the value of q. Therefore, $q^2 = 0.09$. According to the Hardy-Weinberg equation, $1 = p + q$.

$1 = p + 0.3$.
$p = 0.7$
$p^2 = 0.49$
Next, plug q^2 and p^2 into the equation $1 = p^2 + 2pq + q^2$.

$1 = 0.49 + 2pq + 0.09$ (where 2pq is the number of heterozygotes).
$1 = 0.58 + 2pq$
$2pq = 0.42$
Multiply by 100 to get the percent of heterozygotes, 42%.

140. A clownfish is protected by the sea anemone's tentacles. In turn, the anemone receives uneaten food from the clownfish. This is an example of... (Skill 0027)(Average Rigor)

A.   mutualism.
B.   parasitism.
C.   commensalisms.
D.   competition.

A. Neither the clownfish nor the anemone cause harmful effects towards one another and they both benefit from their relationship. Mutualism is when two species that occupy a similar space benefit from their relationship.

141. All of the following are density-independent factors that affect a population except... (Skill 0028)(Easy Rigor)

A.   temperature.
B.   rainfall.
C.   predation.
D.   soil nutrients.

C. As a population increases, the competition for resources is intense and the growth rate declines. This is a density-dependent factor. An example of this would be predation. Density-independent factors affect the population regardless of its size. Examples of density-independent factors are rainfall, temperature, and soil nutrients.

142. Primary succession occurs after... (Skill 0028)(Average Rigor)

A.   nutrient enrichment.
B.   a forest fire.
C.   bare rock is exposed after a water table recedes.
D.   a housing development is built.

C. Primary succession occurs where life never existed before, such as flooded areas or a new volcanic island. It is only after the water recedes that the rock is able to support new life.

143. If DDT were present in an ecosystem, which of the following organisms would have the highest concentration in its system? (Skill 0028)(Rigorous)

A.   grasshopper
B.   eagle
C.   frog
D.   crabgrass

B. Chemicals and pesticides accumulate as you move up the food chain. Tertiary consumers have more accumulated toxins than animals at the bottom of the food chain.

144. Which biome is the most prevalent on Earth? (Skill 0028)(Easy Rigor)

A.   marine
B.   desert
C.   savanna
D.   tundra

A.   The marine biome covers 75% of the Earth. This biome is organized by the depth of water.

145. Which of the following is not an abiotic factor? (Skill 0028)(Average Rigor)

A.   temperature
B.   rainfall
C.   soil quality
D.   bacteria

D. Abiotic factors are non-living aspects of an ecosystem. Bacteria is an example of a biotic factor—a living thing.

146. High humidity and temperature stability are present in which of the following biomes? (Skill 0028)(Easy Rigor)

A.   taiga
B.   deciduous forest
C.   desert
D.   tropical rain forest

D. A tropical rain forest is located near the equator. Its temperature is a constant 25 degrees C and the humidity is high due to the rainfall that exceeds 200 cm per year.

147. **Which trophic level has the highest ecological efficiency?**
(Skill 0028)(Rigorous)

A.   decomposers
B.   producers
C.   tertiary consumers
D.   secondary consumers

B. The amount of energy that is transferred between trophic levels is called the ecological efficiency. The visual of this is represented in a pyramid of productivity. The producers are the most efficient and are at the bottom of this pyramid.

148. **All of the following gasses made up the primitive atmosphere except...**
(Skill 0029)(Rigorous)

A.   ammonia.
B.   methane.
C.   oxygen.
D.   hydrogen.

C. In the 1920's, Oparin and Haldane were to first to theorize that the primitive atmosphere was a reducing atmosphere with no oxygen. The atmosphere was rich in hydrogen, methane, water, and ammonia.

149. **Which term is not associated with the water cycle?**
(Skill 0029)(Easy Rigor)

A.   precipitation
B.   transpiration
C.   fixation
D.   evaporation

C. Water is recycled through the processes of evaporation and precipitation. Transpiration is the evaporation of water from leaves. Fixation is not associated with the water cycle.

150. **In the growth of a population, the increase is exponential until carrying capacity is reached. This is represented by a(n)... (Skill 0030)(Rigorous)**

A.   S curve.
B.   J curve.
C.   M curve.
D.   L curve.

A. An exponentially growing population starts off with little change and then rapidly increases. The graphic representation of this growth curve has the appearance of a "J". However, as the carrying capacity of the exponentially growing population is reached, the growth rate begins to slow down and level off. The graphic representation of this growth curve has the appearance of an "S".

XAMonline, INC. 21 Orient Ave. Melrose, MA 02176

Toll Free number 800-509-4128

TO ORDER Fax 781-662-9268 OR www.XAMonline.com

MASSACHUSETTS TEST FOR EDUCATOR LICENTURE
- MTEL - 2008

PO#   Store/School:

Address 1:

Address 2 (Ship to other):

City, State Zip

Credit card number_____-_____-_____-_____   expiration_____

EMAIL _____

PHONE   **FAX**

ISBN	TITLE	Qty	Retail	Total
978-1-58197-287-0	MTEL Communication and Literacy Skills 01		$27.95	
978-1-58197-876-6	MTEL General Curriculum (formerly Elementary) 03		$28.95	
978-1-58197-607-8	MTEL History 06 (Social Science)		$59.95	
978-1-58197-283-2	MTEL English 07		$59.95	
978-1-58197-349-5	MTEL Mathematics 09		$32.95	
978-1-58197-881-0	MTEL General Science 10		$59.95	
978-1-58197-684-7	MTEL Physics 11		$59.95	
978-1-58197-883-4	MTEL Chemistry 12		$59.95	
978-1-58197-884-1	MTEL Biology 13		$59.95	
978-1-58197-683-0	MTEL Earth Science 14		$59.95	
978-1-58197-676-2	MTEL Early Childhood 02		$73.50	
978-1-58197-893-3	MTEL Visual Art Sample Test 17		$15.00	
978-1-58197-8988	MTEL Political Science/ Political Philosophy 48		$59.95	
978-1-58197-886-5	MTEL Physical Education 22		$59.95	
978-1-58197-887-2	MTEL French Sample Test 26		$15.00	
978-1-58197-888-9	MTEL Spanish 28		$59.95	
978-1-58197-889-6	MTEL Middle School Mathematics 47		$59.95	
978-1-58197-890-2	MTEL Middle School Humanities 50		$59.95	
978-1-58197-891-9	MTEL Middle School Mathematics-Science 51		$59.95	
978-1-58197-266-5	MTEL Foundations of Reading 90 (requirement all El. Ed)		$59.95	
			SUBTOTAL	
			Ship	$8.25
			TOTAL	